P9-AAY-782

How Good Is Your School?

Program Evaluation for Secondary Schools

by
William Georgiades

EDUCATIONAL LEADERSHIP LIBRARY
SCHOOL MANAGEMENT INSTITUTE
located on the
University of South Florida Campus
and funded by

THE NATIONAL ASSOCIATION OF SECONDARY SCHOOL PRINCIPALS
RESTON, VA.

Copyright 1978
All Rights Reserved
The National Association of Secondary School Principals
1904 Association Drive, Reston, Virginia 22091

ISBN 0-88210-087-4

Contents

Foreword

How Good Is Your School? is the third of four reports that describe the Model Schools Project. Launched in 1971 by NASSP under the direction of J. Lloyd Trump with a generous grant from the Danforth Foundation, the five-year Project was an attempt by everyone involved to find a better way of educating the nation's youth.

Our first publication, *A School for Everyone,* describes the MSP design for secondary schools, one that offers a variety of choices with appropriate guidance and controls. The second, the November 1977 *NASSP Bulletin,* contains articles by 16 MSP principals who describe what happened in their schools. Our final report will describe the change process that can improve any school.

This third publication, written by William Georgiades, professor of education at the University of Southern California and associate director of the MSP, describes the program evaluation system utilized during the Project. The emphasis is on criterion-referenced evaluation, but other methods are also discussed.

How Good Is Your School? appropriately reflects the conviction that the primary purpose of evaluation is to assist students, teachers, and administrators to determine the kinds of methods and materials which will facilitate learning wherever it takes place. This report of the Model Schools Project is especially significant because it emphasizes the total spectrum of evaluation, starting with the institution, its understandings and commitment, and concluding with the product—the affective, skills, and cognitive learnings of students.

Although simple answers and evaluative techniques are not easily devised, we believe this book will help readers determine what kinds of evaluation are needed to assess the myriad goals of today's secondary schools.

Owen B. Kiernan
NASSP Executive Director

Preface

Thirty-two junior and senior high schools in 1969 embarked on a five-year project designed to provide individualized learning strategies for their students. Called the Model Schools Project, the program focused on quality education in a way never so systematically undertaken by educators before.

Stemming from the Project is this book, a summary of the efforts, both successful and unsuccessful. It evaluates the many facets of each participating school's program, structure, and people. It attempts to raise questions about the ways we assess the *quality* of a school. It presents the exciting story of the evaluative findings from the 32 participating junior and senior high schools that voluntarily committed themselves to a highly individualized learning model for students.

Sponsored by the National Association of Secondary School Principals with partial support from the Danforth Foundation, the Model Schools Project was unique in that it attempted to look at all aspects of school programs and the ways in which they interrelate. It functioned with a relatively small central staff in order to place major responsibilities on the schools for developing their own programs in relationship to the prescribed model. While schools participated voluntarily, the majority of their staffs indicated a commitment as did their respective boards of education.

The purpose of this book is to provide new options and directions which may be used by persons interested in assessing the quality of their schools' offerings. This report reflects a sensitivity to current needs for improved evaluation in all aspects of schools, ranging from the most conventional to the most innovative. The reader will learn new and more effective ways to evaluate school programs.

W.G.

1

The Truth about Evaluation

During the twentieth century, what evaluation mythologies has American education perpetuated? How can education be evaluated through the use of a balanced evaluative design, not by myths?

A MAJOR REASON FOR the abrupt decline of many innovative educational efforts during the past decade is the failure of their proponents to document adequately claims relating to pupil growth and progress. Skeptical publics of all generations, including those within the educational profession, demand evidence beyond mere claims by proponents of new models for education.

The Myths of Evaluation

For quite some time, American education has perpetuated many myths relating to evaluation. Evaluative techniques and ways of determining quality familiar to the public include simplistic measures such as the results of norm-referenced tests, numbers of volumes in a library, degrees

1

held by teachers, class size, standardized test results, per pupil expenditures, the newness of a building, teacher salaries, scholarship winners, and athletic trophies.

Do these measures accurately reflect the quality of a school program? Let's take a further look at some of these myths.

It is relatively easy for a school to purchase a norm-referenced test, administer it to a student body, and then publicly to announce its results. The test results are favorable, of course, if the students are culturally oriented toward the items included on the tests. Invariably, these students perform above the so-called national norm. Consequently, it has been good public relations for schools in affluent communities to release information stating that their students are attaining superior scores on norm-referenced tests.

Such information actually tells the community, "Through the environment you have provided, your children are intellectually curious and have the basic skills to master the kinds of information demanded by norm-referenced tests." The results give little indication of the unique contribution (or lack thereof) that a school may have made to a student's growth over a four-year span.

Another poor indicator of quality is the use of quantitative, accrediting criteria. The number of books in a library or degrees held by teachers, for example, give little evidence of the effectiveness of a school program. They reflect the relative affluency and cultural orientation of a community but cannot relate pupil expectancy to pupil achievement. They do little to answer the question of "How good is your school?"

Another myth associated with evaluation is class size. For generations, the public has been told that smaller class sizes will produce more effective pupil learning. However, there is little significant research to support this broad and expansive generalization.

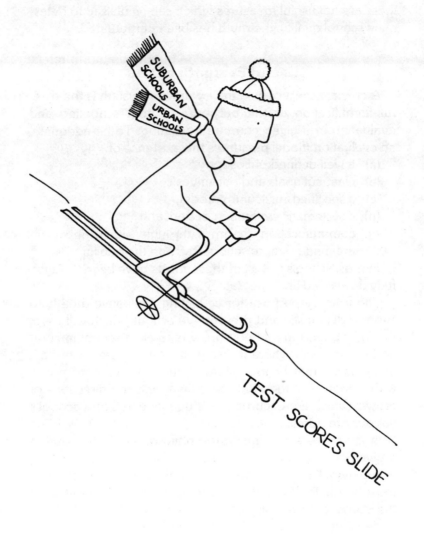

TEST SCORES SLIDE

For decades affluent school districts have prided themselves on such variables as pupil-teacher ratios, dollars spent per pupil, and teacher salaries. In spite of evidence that these are not useful measures which can be utilized to determine school quality, the myth has been perpetuated.

Useful Evaluative Data

A crucial aspect of a sound evaluation system is the careful identification of the purposes of both schooling and evaluation in a given community setting. To be adequate, an evaluation model presumes the existence of:

(a) a well-defined philosophy,
(b) clear-cut goals and objectives,
(c) a specified curriculum model,
(d) a systematic evaluation design, and
(e) communication channels through which the results are made clear to school staff and the public.

In most schools not all of these facets have been thoughtfully developed and integrated.

The primary purpose for collecting evaluative data is to support diagnostic and prescriptive actions which will assist the individual student in his growth; to aid a school in comparing itself with where it was yesterday, where it is today, and where it may be in the future; and to provide the public with evidence of the kinds of growth and the directions of growth which are occurring as students enroll in a school's various programs.

In the process of defining the philosophy of schooling in a given community, such steps as a needs assessment, an occupational analysis, and a survey of parental expectations must be made. It is important for educators to know what the community perceives to be its unique needs and the underlying purposes and functions of education. Also, it is critical that a school be evaluated in terms of its goals rather than how it compares with other schools in its own or other communities.

Another facet of evaluation is the degree to which a curriculum model has been identified and implemented. (We refer here to the courses, activities, methodologies, resources, staffing, school climate, facilities, etc., of a school's program.) Some schools have developed college-oriented curriculum models that are measured by norm-referenced testing, but such measurements are limited in scope.

Following the identification of a community's expectations of its schools, the development of clear-cut goals and objectives, and the organization of a curriculum model, a systematic evaluation design must be organized, including the two recognized types: formative (evaluation as change occurs) and summative (evaluation of final results).

The evaluative design used in the Model Schools Project consisted of

- understanding and commitment of the participants to the Project's design,
- the analysis of criterion-referenced data in relation to program objectives,
- the adoption and following of a curriculum model,
- the use of the diagnostic-prescriptive-implementation-evaluative cycle,
- the use of norm-based data, and
- the use of competent outside visitors to the schools to observe certain identified areas and make reports on them.

Finally, if the purposes of evaluation are to be realized, open channels of communication between school staff and public are essential. The public has every right to expect accurate reports on the progress their children are making toward the goals and objectives of education in their community. Such communication must indicate the ways in which the process of diagnosis-prescription-implementation-evaluation (DPIE) has been utilized to assist individual pupil growth.

The DPIE process should also aid professionals in reporting to parents and students those areas of growth and weakness the student has exhibited in a given time frame. It is much more definitive to indicate to interested parents where a student is on a growth continuum—what he has accomplished and can do—than to try to explain the elusive nature of an A, B, C, D, or F grade.

Whys and Wherefores of Evaluation

Evaluative efforts like those undertaken in the Model Schools Project focus on the accurate reporting of student growth. The development of evaluative designs, a time-consuming task, for all areas of the curriculum and for all the different aspects of the school cannot be accomplished simultaneously. Nonetheless, many of the 32 participating schools made extraordinary progress during the five years of the Project. The next chapter shows how they made progress.

The purpose of the entire book, however, is to present evaluative designs for schools who wish to assess more accurately where they are. It offers suggested evaluative models as well as findings from the Model Schools Project. At the close of each chapter are suggested activities that may assist readers who seek to enhance the evaluative process.

Suggested Activities

1. Identify the unique purposes of schooling in your community. Such purposes could be clarified through community surveys, citizen interviews, informal discussion groups. How can these purposes best be achieved?

2. What curriculum model is being followed in your school? What were its origins and how was it implemented?

6

3. Speak with administrators, teachers, or other knowledgeable individuals in your school who are responsible for evaluating the school's educational programs. Discuss how goals and objectives are determined, how they are being measured, and what attempts are being made to meet such goals and objectives.

4. Review a recent copy of a regional accreditation report. What criteria were applied to evaluate the school's programs?

5. Participate in a district or local school needs assessment survey. Review carefully the student population, its expectancies, and its growth during the time enrolled in the secondary school.

2

Assessing the Quality of a School

Concern for quality schools and quality education was a major stimulus for the implementation and organization of the Model Schools Project. Isn't the need for quality education in conventional schools just as evident as it is in innovative schools?

WHILE THE NEEDS OF individuals vary substantially, societies and communities have certain common goals in maintaining their schools. These aims are based heavily on the cognitive achievement and the affective development of our youth. American society for many years has expended considerable energy in providing a system of schooling for the majority of its citizens. Concerns about quantity, however, have sometimes overshadowed questions of quality.

Before a school can measure the quality of its educational program, it must define quality in terms of its community, its population, and its unique environment. Anyone attempting to define quality must do so in terms of specified demands, interests, and objectives.

While no one can present a panacea for determining quality, this book does present new options and new directions which can help persons interested in assessing the quality of their schools' offerings. The data gathered were accumulated through the use of external auditors, from private studies, from a wide range of self-assessment techniques, and through the involvement of paid observers selected by schools participating in the Model Schools Project. Nothing in this book is intended to say that the techniques and data gathered are good or bad.

In attempting to measure the total spectrum of the objectives of quality schooling, the Project was faced with many limitations. Not all the data gathered grew out of tightly systematic and rigidly controlled experimental designs. Some of the data are affective and therefore indicate how persons felt. And to some extent, evaluation was limited by the degree to which various schools were able to implement the Model.

In answering the question of quality, the Model Schools Project gave considerable weight to what teachers and other persons immersed in the Project believed to be the results of their own experimentation. Accurate descriptions by persons involved in this Project were often as important as the elaborate analysis of achievement data.

Conventional and Innovative Schools

In many respects terms like "conventional" and "innovative" are elusive. By conventional, the writer refers to those schools which have maintained ongoing traditional programs via standardized, 50-minute periods of study each day. Usually, conventional schools have not made provisions for individual students to proceed at their own rate of learning. Consequently, many conventional schools have retained a lock-step educational structure with the accumulation of credits based upon the amount of time a student has spent in a given subject field. In addition, conventional schools have usually not used diagnosis as a means of prescribing instructional methodology and instructional materials.

On the other hand, innovative high schools are defined as those which have sought to offer credit based upon performance via the use of a diagnostic-prescriptive-implementation-evaluation cycle appropriate for each student. Time spent in studying a given subject field is not germane to the granting of student credit in such schools.

Components of the Model Schools Project

Out of a large number of junior and senior high schools that showed interest in being a part of the Project, 34 were actually selected for participation; four of these eventually decided not to continue as members and two new schools were added. There were 32 schools involved when the Project closed.

Each school agreed to implement the following aspects of the Model as rapidly as feasible:

- The needs and competencies of each teacher would be diagnosed. Consequently, both instructional and clerical aid time would be provided on a weekly basis. Thus, teachers would work cooperatively in using differentiated staffing.

- Instruction and learning would take place in large groups (typically two or more conventional classes), small groups (eight to 20 students), and independent study (students learning at differential rates appropriate for each).

  a. There was to be one large-group presentation and one small-group discussion in each area of the curriculum every week.

  b. Most students were to have upwards of 60 percent individualized study time per week.

- Students were to receive curricular instruction every week of every year in all of the following eight areas (a ninth being religion in private schools): English, fine arts, health and recreation, mathematics, foreign cultures, practical arts, social studies, and science.

- Learning was to be individualized with much use of packaged units of study, each offering a variety of learning activities to match different learning styles.

- The principal was to spend three-quarters of his or her time as the school's instructional leader. This practice was made possible by the development of the supervisory-management team in which all persons with administrative responsibilities would work cooperatively.

- Conventional grading was to be downplayed in favor of actual performance descriptions of student growth.

- Students, under a continuous progress arrangement, were to be granted credit for completion of work at natural stopping places rather than at quarters, semesters, or at the end of conventional school years.

- Grade levels were to be essentially abolished.

- All curricular areas were to have resource centers.

- All teachers were to have semi-private or private offices.

- Every teacher was to be an adviser to 20 or 30 students throughout the students' years in school, meeting with them daily to plot their use of school time.

Schools were selected from various parts of the United States and Canada, including rural, urban, and suburban areas. Some were impoverished districts; others were affluent. The key prerequisite was strong interest in changing education from a conventional six- or seven-period day into a flexible one that offered more natural learning styles.

11

The next chapter focuses on understanding and commitment as a prerequisite to evaluation. Without understanding that commitment, one may be evaluating a traditional program with a new name.

Suggested Activities

1. Read several of the numerous articles describing the development and organization of the Model Schools Project. These can be found in the *Bulletin* of the National Association of Secondary School Principals (1969-1975).

2. Rent the film "Answers and Questions" (1968) or the film "Tomorrow's Schools: Images and Plans (1972). National Association of Secondary School Principals, 1904 Association Drive, Reston, Va., 22091.

3. Discuss with local school officials their recent attempts to individualize and personalize the educational programs in your community. What attempts have succeeded? What attempts have failed? Analyze the reasons for successes and failures. Based on these initial attempts, what goals and objectives are your school district supporting for the continued development of an individualized educational program?

4. Using the diagnosis-prescriptive-implementation-evaluation cycle assess where your school is in meeting individual school needs.

3

Understanding and Commitment

The Model Schools Project was based on the idea that commitment to total change would produce significant gains in pupil learning and in the professionalization of teaching. It stressed the interrelationships of all three aspects of the teacher-learning environment (programs, people, and structure). It was based on the assumption that to change one of these components would be unproductive unless the other two aspects of the learning environment were also directly involved in the innovation or change process. What were the MSP research findings with respect to understanding of and commitment to change?

FOR MORE THAN A decade, school systems have described innovative programs with such terms as team teaching, continuous progress education, differentiated staffing, open schools, school-management teams, and independent study. These labels have plagued the educational scene but they have done little to influence actual classroom practice. Behind the classroom door there has been little change in teacher behavior, primarily because there has been little understanding of or commitment to the new concepts and ideas which these terms imply.

13

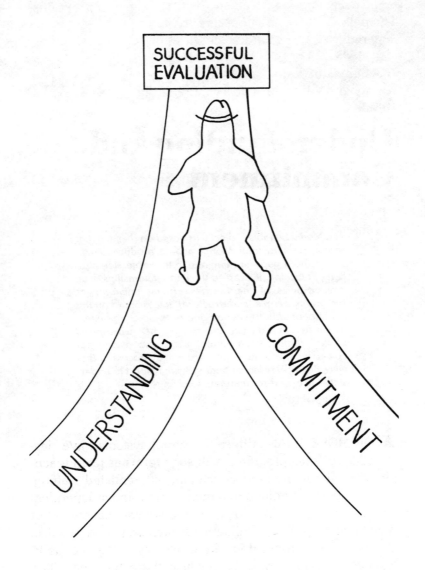

Many of the so-called team-teaching programs have really been "part-time teaching," or "turn-teaching" designs. The philosophy of "It's your turn today, my turn tomorrow" may reduce the teacher workload, but it is hardly consistent with the concept of cooperative teaching.

As implemented, team teaching is nothing more than a boring experience that tests the endurance of a captive secondary student audience. Often one sees 60, 70, or even 100 adolescents sitting in a hot, stuffy auditorium, being lectured to in an abstract, remote fashion. The lack of understanding of the purpose of large-group instruction has been one of the major deterrents in effective application of this concept.

The purposes and functions of small-group discussions and interactions have been equally misunderstood. Sadly, teacher-talk in groups of eight to ten students is often just as prevalent as in conventional-sized classes. For decades good traditional programs have sought ways to implement vital, meaningful, small-group relationships, but until an in-depth understanding of this concept and method takes place, teacher implementation will be ineffectual.

Independent study has also been a major concern of educators. How can students learn to develop a sensitivity for and an ability to assume a major responsibility for their own individual development?

Implementation of the concept has enabled teachers to have additional time away from students, but it has not served the important function of assisting students in "learning how to learn." The concept is sound but it fails in practice through a misunderstanding of its possibilities and its limitations.

Beyond understanding new concepts and ideas in education is the critical factor of commitment. The commitment of a school, its students, teachers, supervisory-management team, and community to a clearly defined model of education is essential.

Commitment in conventional schools has shown itself through such financial considerations as class size, the number of books in a library, and the salaries paid the school staff. Commitment, so translated, is often confused with quality education. What little research is available does not support these "commitments" as key factors in the development of quality education. Commitment, too, has been confused with the things of education rather than with the ideas, the purposes, and the philosophy of schooling.

If meaningful understanding of and commitment to a better education are to emerge, new ways of looking at schools must be examined carefully. When community groups and trustee organizations asked questions about school quality in the past, the answers were stated simplistically and categorically on the basis of quantity standards. For generations, the public was told that if it wanted a superior educational program for its children and young people, schools would have to reduce class size, increase teachers' salaries, place more books in libraries, etc. While these may be meritorious, they give no guarantee of quality schooling.

Numerous efforts were undertaken during the Model Schools Project to determine the levels of understanding of staff, students, and segments of the community. The commitment of these same groups to the goals and objectives of the Project was also assessed. The most extensive study was undertaken in 1972 by B. Flavian Udinsky, James W. Keefe, and Jack L. Housden. It was based on data collected in the spring of 1971 from 29 of the secondary schools in the Project. The study was replicated in 1974 (using data collected in the spring of 1973) by George O'Brien.

Two other studies illustrative of different but effective approaches to documenting understanding and commitment to the Model were undertaken. The first of these assessed the program at Bishop Carroll High School, Calgary, Alberta, Canada. This assessment was designed and administered by Newton Metfessel of the University of Southern California. The second consisted of a series of participant-observation studies made by external auditors during the first year of the Project.

What were the findings of these four studies?

Udinsky-Keefe-Housden Study

The Udinsky-Keefe-Housden (UKH) study used a Thurstonian-type questionnaire to measure the attitudes and understandings of the administration, the teachers, and the students toward the Model. This initial survey asked: (1) What do you like best about the Model Schools Project? and why? (2) If you could change (only) one thing about the Model Schools Project, what would you change? and why? The scales finally used to measure understanding and commitment toward the Model are found in Appendix A (Items 44-63).

Twenty-nine high schools participating in the Model Schools Project during its first two years (1969-71) were involved in the study. Every principal and teacher contributed to the study, whereas students were randomly selected from each school.

Teachers, students, and principals responded to a survey questionnaire evaluating the implementation of seven areas of the Extent of Teacher Role Change (ETRC) as well as identifying selected characteristics of the MSP program (CMSP). Teachers and students also responded to questionnaire items designed to measure Attitudes Toward the MSP (ATMSP). Finally, teachers alone responded to forced-choice items identified as the major factors Contributing to or Inhibiting Full Implementation of the desired MSP teacher role change (CIFIC, Appendix A, Items 64 and 65).

17

Among the findings in this study was the fact that teacher-identified attitude scores correlated highly with role change scores in 16 of the 29 schools. This would seem to indicate that appropriate kinds of preservice and inservice involvement did produce understanding of and commitment to the Model. However, preservice and inservice programs in and of themselves did not necessarily result in understanding when attitudes were negative about the Model Schools Project.

The "contagious" nature of change was also seen in that student attitudes correlated with teacher-role-change scores in 12 of the 29 schools. When teacher attitudes were positive and there was a sense of commitment, teacher roles more readily changed to be consistent with the new Model, and student attitudes also became more positive.

When the attitude scores for all teachers within a given school were combined into a composite teacher attitude index and compared with a similar index of role change for the school, some interesting findings resulted. There was a slight relationship between teacher and student attitudes toward the Model Schools Project and the extent of teacher role change perceived in the school. In the O'Brien study, conducted two years later, both of these comparisons were significant. It appears that with time and commitment, understanding developed. This understanding was reflected both in attitudes and in the ways in which teachers' roles changed. With time, there was no decline in commitment and an actual increase in the level of understanding.

A second conclusion was that schools are slow to change, particularly if the change affects many parts of the system. Piecemeal changes—a little team teaching, a small dose of differentiated staffing (through the use of aides), a few new elective courses—are easy to introduce, but large-scale change is resisted by a school's various social structures.

Teachers and principals after attending inservice workshops would return home highly enthusiastic, but then

18

would be unable to introduce substantive change into their local settings. Winning acceptance of one's peers, giving leadership to one's colleagues, and effectively communicating the nature of anticipated change to community persons were areas in which implementation efforts often collapsed.

A third significant conclusion of this study was that failure to adequately diagnose local variables delayed the implementation of the Model in many communities. Contrasts among inner city, suburban, and rural schools had a dramatic impact on the speed and degree of implementation of the Model over the five-year span of the Project.

A fourth conclusion of the Udinsky-Keefe-Housden study was that the principal cannot assume that he or she knows the extent of curricular innovation taking place in his or her school. The complexities of a modern junior or senior high school make it extremely difficult for a principal to get an accurate "reading" of what is taking place. Some principals tend to see that which they want to see, not what is actually happening. Perhaps the "survival instinct" of principals is such that they must maintain an optimistic posture. Teachers, not having to relate as directly to community persons, may be more temperate in their claims and less public relations conscious.

A fifth major conclusion dealt with the teachers' perceptions of the principal's leadership activities. It is not sufficient for a principal to give approval or lip-service to curricular innovations; rather, he or she must be deeply involved in developing and aiding the intended changes. The principal must participate actively in inservice activities, critique progress personally on a daily basis, and facilitate teacher needs for materials, plan modifications, etc. Where principals were "up to their eyeballs," so to speak, with the curricular changes, teachers seemed to work harder and obtain greater results and satisfaction.

A sixth conclusion was that time and change do not work in any fixed discernible way. Some schools in the Project were radically different after one year, others took two years, and still others did not change significantly until near the conslution of the five-year Project. Changing schools is highly individualistic and dependent upon numerous local variables.

A final pertinent conclusion was that schools with a high degree of Model implementation provided students with a wider variety of avenues for learning and had a greater degree of teacher-role change. Lecturing or talking at students diminished while various kinds of small groups and independent study activities increased substantially. Thus, teachers spent less time talking and pupils spent more time learning.

The O'Brien Study

The O'Brien study was conducted at the end of the fourth year of the Project. It was similar in approach and organization to the Udinsky-Keefe-Housden study, but only 20 of the 29 schools involved in the UKH study voluntarily participated this time.[1]

The study indicated a significant relationship between teacher and student attitudes and the perceptions of role change. With experience and a subsequent lowering of the level of frustration, teachers and schools implemented the model more effectively and extensively. In addition, there were some indications of a higher degree of success recognized and appreciated by the local community. The O'Brien study also indicated that those teachers who implemented

---

1. Some schools received the materials too late in the school year to participate in this evaluation; others chose not to. Since participation in the Project was voluntary, pressures were not exerted to force schools to utilize these evaluative materials.

the Model more diligently had more favorable attitudes about it.

In the O'Brien study, students in MSP schools with a high degree of Model implementation reported that their parents had an understanding of the Project's goals and objectives well beyond those in the low-ranking schools. Also, 71 percent of the teachers in high-ranking schools rated parent attitudes "somewhat highly favorable" whereas only 36 percent of teachers in low-ranking schools rated them similarly. Apparently, parental understanding and regard for a model is a concomitant of a more successful level of implementation.

On the other hand, there was very little difference between the attitudes of students in high- and low-ranking schools with respect to the Model Schools Project. Eighty-nine percent of students in high-ranking schools and 84 percent in the low-ranking schools rated the MSP program from "somewhat better" to "far better" than conventional programs. Such strong positive reactions could result from an "innovative bias" operating. Students in such schools may be intrigued with the idea that something very special is going on. Another possibility is that student regard for their own school may be quite independent of teacher implementation of a given innovative design. Whether a school is highly or only slightly innovative may not affect student morale appreciably.

The O'Brien study indicated a somewhat higher level of understanding of and commitment to the Model on the part of both parents and students than the Udinsky-Keefe-Housden survey found. Where professional implementation and understanding were high, parental attitudes were also high.

Without understanding and commitment on the part of the professionals who manage and operate the school, one can hardly expect understanding and commitment on the part of the public and students. Both the O'Brien and the Udinsky-Keefe-Housden studies supported this generalization.

The Metfessel Study

Longitudinal data similar to those in the previously mentioned studies were also collected at Bishop Carroll High School in Calgary, Alberta, Canada for the 1972-74 school years. This evaluation was conducted by an external evaluation team from the University of Southern California and external auditors from the Alberta Provincial Department of Education and the University of Alberta.

Prior to initiating the evaluation, the philosophy, concepts, and rationale of the Model Schools Project were carefully reviewed by the auditors with each member of the school staff. One hundred percent of the staff indicated agreement.

The conceptualization of change was phrased in the context of humanizing the program. From this grew the following premises for organizing an individualized instructional system:

- A school's environment should encourage interaction between students and their peers, between students and teachers, and among professional staff and the larger community.

- Curriculum should be related to the "real" world rather than disassociated from life. Instruction should nurture independence, provide opportunities beyond the regular curriculum, and encourage maximum use of resources. The individual requirements of each student should be met at his/her level of ability, achievement, and rate of progress.

- Classroom instructional methods and organization patterns should reflect effective techniques for coping with the individual differences of the students.

22

- Learning in youth is internalized as a continuing process. Along with this process is the need for guidance of each individual's interests and needs.
- Multiple interactions and multiple instructional exposure should provide the framework for motivation.
- A continuous state of evaluation and change should support the program. Change must be internalized by those involved.
- Individualization should promote new uses of time, space, numbers, and money without necessarily additional funds.

In the Bishop Carroll program, measurable objectives were developed and identified; and student progress was then measured for these objectives. The three most important cognitive and affective objectives were selected for the 1972-74 evaluation.

Two teacher objectives were also identified in addition to student objectives to be evaluated during the 1972-74 school years. Then 450 students (1972) and 420 students (1973) were evaluated for each student objective, and 31 teachers (1972) and 30 teachers (1973) were evaluated for each teacher objective. Findings of the evaluation studies to measure progress toward both teacher and student objectives were:

1. Cognitive objective for students in the area of method: By the end of the 1973-74 school year, a minimum of 80 percent of the groups in each grade level would attain not less than a mean average of 105 on characteristics of individualized instruction as indicated by the Process Index of Individualized Instruction. (Note: Level I is equivalent to grade 10, level II to grade 11, level III to grade 12).

The Process Index of Individualized Instruction rated respondents on a Likert-type scale in four general categories: effective small group discussion, persistence in work, effective self-evaluation, and selecting independent projects. The Index was intended to provide evidence as to whether an effective environment had been established for individualized instruction and whether students were taking advantage of that environment. This objective was attained by 100 percent of the groups responding on levels, I, II, and III.

2. Affective objective for students in the area of organization: By the end of the 1973-74 school year a minimum of 80 percent of the groups in each level would obtain not less than a mean average of 120 in the assessment of the organizational environment as indicated by the High School Organizational Environment Inventory.

This inventory measured eight affective variables, again looking at the organization of the school, to determine whether the environment supported motivation, affective climate, pursuit of interests, self-direction, self-expression, concern for the person (humanization), stimulating learning opportunities (structure), and life-oriented learning (philosophy). This inventory was not an attitudinal scale but an evaluation of the affective processes that make up the school organizational climate. It used a Likert-type scale to rate items such as the following:

—The materials and instruction seem to be at the appropriate learning level for most students, neither boring nor frustrating. Students are encouraged to develop their individual talents and interests.

—The environment encourages interaction between students and classmates, students and the staff, and students and the community.

The objective was attained by 100 percent of the groups in grades 10, 11, and 12 at Bishop Carroll.

3. Cognitive objective for students in the area of method/facility: By the end of the 1973-74 school year, a minimum of 80 percent of the groups in each level would attain not less than a mean average of 52 on the utilization of human and learning resources as measured by the Study Habits and Skills Test.

This instrument rated students on how well they took advantage of teacher help in the school and how well they used print and non-print materials in the school resource centers. In 1972-73, only 66 percent of the students were perceived to be at this objective. In 1973-74, all of them scored above 52.

4. Cognitive objective for teachers in the area of method: This objective was identical to objective one but was geared to teachers rather than students. It also used the Process Index of Individualized Instruction. Teacher scores on this process index rose from a median of 116.5 in 1972-73 to a median score of 131.5 in 1973-74. Twenty-eight of 30 teachers showed results above the criterion level.

5. The affective objective was the same as objective two, but geared to teachers. It used the High School Organization Environment Inventory once again. Teacher scores on this Inventory rose from a median of 144.5 in 1972-73 to a median score of 169.0 in 1973-74. All 30 participating teachers showed results above the criterion level.

These five objectives, and others reported in earlier chapters, provided extensive, detailed evaluation of the learning environment at Bishop Carroll High School. The evaluative methods asked the question, "Are the goals of the Project being implemented?" As such, they provided a picture of the process of implementation during the actual formative years of the program. The data collected were not only valuable as feedback for the staff but as a graphic description of the strengths and weaknesses in this high school's progress toward the Model.

Other Findings

As noted previously, the teachers responded to two instruments which had also been given the students. These were the "Process Index of Individualized Instruction" and the "High School Organizational Environment Inventory." These instruments, selected by the Metfessel evaluation team, were utilized to measure not only progress toward the stated objectives of the program but also to measure commitment to and understanding of those objectives. The teachers were also administered a "Meaning of Words Inventory," which contained different bipolar adjectives than the instrument provided the students.

The teacher scores on the "Process Index of Individualized Instruction" rose from a median of 116.5 in 1972-73 to a median score of 131.5 in the 1973-74 year. Thus, 28 of the school's 30 teachers perceived a significant improvement in student adaptation to individualized instructional modes. Students were more consistently following through on their work, they were doing a better job of self-evaluation, they were more effective in small-group discussions, and they utilized independent study time more efficiently.

The teacher scores on the "High School Organizational Environment Inventory" rose from a median of 144.5 in 1972-73 to a median score of 169.0 in the 1973-74 year. This meant that all 30 teachers perceived themselves to be more effective in using the various components of the Model, including large group, small group, and student independent study. All felt that they were significantly better in organizing learning environments for individualized instruction.

Meaning of Words Inventory

Each term in Table I has nine pairs of bipolar adjectives to which the teachers reacted with a degree of positive or negative feeling. For instance, teachers were asked about such factors as working climate and morale; shared decision making; internal school communication; school-community relations; the use of instructional aides; the effectiveness of large group, small group, and independent study; and progress toward humanizing the curriculum.

Each pair of bipolar adjectives had a possible value of seven points. A value of four was required to indicate a positive reaction for this evaluation. The values expressed in the table consist of the average values given to the nine bipolar adjectives with respect to each reference term. The table reflects that teachers, for the most part, had a more positive attitude toward the changes that were occurring as they became further immersed in the five-year Project.

Both student and teacher results at Bishop Carroll indicated a high level of understanding of and commitment to the goals of the Model Schools Project. In addition, both students and teachers showed highly positive attitudes. The teacher "Meaning of Words Inventory" indicated a positive response in all categories for both the 1972-73 and the 1973-74 school year evaluations, excepting only school-community relations in 1972-73. In addition, all mean scores showed increases from 1973 to 1974 except the category of instructional assistants which remained virtually the same.

These results indicated a high level of commitment and understanding at Bishop Carroll High School toward the Project. In carefully examining the gestalt of change, with particular focus on understanding and commitment, the

27

TABLE 1
Faculty Average Scores on Meaning of Words Inventory
(Value above 4 is positive reaction)

Variables	Average Score 1972-1973	Average Score 1973-1974
Working Climate	5.33	5.73
Shared Decision Making	4.65	4.88
Within School Communication	4.25	4.52
School-Community Relations	3.95	4.50
Instructional Assistant	5.56	5.53
Students	5.11	5.62
Large-Group Presentation	4.50	4.50
Small-Group Discussion	3.97	5.01
Independent Study	5.05	5.40
Teaching in an MSP School	5.67	6.01
Humanizing the Curriculum	5.11	5.53
Teachers' Morale	4.99	5.47
Student Progress in an MSP School	4.31	5.18
My Professional Growth	5.49	5.61
Individualized Instruction	5.22	5.57
Student Self-Evaluation	4.39	4.68
Resources and Materials	4.66	5.29
Inservice Training	4.16	4.91
Differentiated Staffing	5.10	5.52
Continuous Progress	5.12	5.61

evaluators recommended this school "as a model for educators implementing tenets of individualization of instruction." Bishop Carroll came to be recognized by all as the single best example of the Model Schools Project and ideally what a high school today should be like for boys and girls.

This type of evaluation, while incorporating the use of norm-referenced and criterion-referenced examinations, relied primarily on individualized types of testing. The primary objective of the evaluation model was to assess pupil growth in the light of pupil needs. The focus of the evaluative process was on the use of testing for diagnostic-prescriptive purposes.

Other Studies

Numerous evaluation instruments were used to assess the level of understanding and/or commitment of the school staff in other schools. One such instrument utilized was the Ross Education Scale. This scale presents respondents with 30 statements on ideas and problems about which all educators have beliefs, opinions, and attitudes. It encourages individuals to express their feelings in order to categorize their philosophical leanings in education. The scale yields three indices, two of which deal with the teacher's traditional or progressive bent in working with youth. The use of this and other instruments enabled MSP schools to build a program of inservice with respect to achieving a better understanding of and commitment toward the purposes and goals of the MSP program.

Some MSP schools designed local surveys to assess teacher, instructional aide, clerical staff and/or administrator understanding of and commitment to the various components of the Model. These instruments usually rated teacher or staff perception on a Likert-type scale. Staffs were asked to "agree" or "disagree" with statements such as the following:

—Students are known by teachers and instructional aides on a personal basis.

—The faculty and instructional aides feel a sense of loyalty toward their school.

—The divisional structure helps to create an atmosphere that is conducive to learning.

—Members of the administration are familiar with departmental structures and procedures.

—The individual faculty member has a voice in the decision-making process.

At Pius X High School careful surveys were conducted at the end of each year to assess the attitudes of students, teachers, and aides toward changes in the school program. The surveys first reviewed conditions for learning environments. The majority of both students and teachers felt it was easier to make friends with other students in an individualized instructional program committed to the Model. While 70 percent of the teachers felt that students could be more successful in their work, only 40 percent of the students had a similar perception. On the other hand, 80 percent of the teachers and 75 percent of the students felt that the individualized learning program being followed better enabled a student to learn to think for himself. Ninety-four percent of the teachers and 78 percent of the students felt they were becoming more responsible for their own learning.

Among the interesting findings in the Pius X surveys was the fact that 98 percent of the teachers and 82 percent of the students felt they were learning to work more independently without direct teacher supervision. Eighty-two percent of the teachers and 66 percent of the students felt they were better able to organize their school time. Among the problems encountered in individualizing education was getting assignments done on time. In the Pius X surveys, 25 percent of the teachers and 25 percent of the students felt they were able to complete assignments on time. In relationship to the teacher-adviser role, 78 percent of the teachers and 53 percent of the students felt that they knew their teacher/advisers better than they had in a traditional school situation.

When utilized, these types of inventories helped give a clearer picture of student and teacher perceptions of the Model, their understandings of the Model, and their commitment to the Model.

Another approach to the assessment of teacher commitment to the Model was an expanded form of self-evaluation similar to the teacher evaluation devices previously proposed by the National Association of Secondary School Principals. Teachers were asked a series of questions about instructional classroom discipline and extracurricular responsibilities. They were asked to indicate whether they rated themselves "high," "average," or "low" in the various categories. Data collected dealt with teachers' attitudes about the Model Schools Project, including their knowledge of the Project philosophy, the degree to which their creativity was encouraged, their general cooperation with peers in team planning, their ability and willingness to assume a fair share of the work load, their long-range commitment to the Project, their willingness to work with individual students, and their awareness of the need for sound communication skills.

The preceding techniques were used for diagnostic purposes. Following their use, faculties developed in-service education programs to facilitate their understanding of the Model itself. The evidence indicated that with understanding, commitment grew. The reverse can also be stated, for with commitment understanding seemed much easier.

The next chapter shows how innovative schools use criterion-referenced evaluation as a means of diagnosis and assisting students. It focuses on individual pupil growth rather than collective group growth.

Suggested Activities

1. Discuss the concept of total or "gestalt" change versus the idea of limited or partial change with a teacher, administrator, or professor of education. What are the strengths and the weaknesses of both approaches and what are the implications for understanding and commitment?

2. Plan a visit to a nearby innovative school. What do you perceive to be the nature of understanding and commitment on the part of students, teachers, and administrators? What factors seem the easiest to change? What factors seem the most difficult? Can you offer any reasons for your answers to these questions?

3. Analyze the understanding in your school of purposes, techniques, and methodology of instruction. How much agreement is there among the staff with such approaches to learning? How successful is the school in assisting pupils to achieve their learning objectives?

4. Examine the current literature which describes some of the national efforts to innovate and individualize education. What common understandings seem to influence and direct such efforts?

5. Look at your own school or visit a nearby school. How much student time is spent participating in large-group presentations, in small-group discussions, and in independent or directed study? How much understanding is there of these concepts on the part of both students and teachers? What commitment is there to these concepts?

4

Criterion-Referenced Evaluation

Practical problems arise when a school attempts to translate an educational evaluation theory, such as criterion-referenced evaluation, into practice. Nonetheless, how can criterion-referenced measurement become a meaningful reality as a school attempts to design an individualized curriculum? In what ways did the Model Schools Project utilize criterion-referenced measurement, accountability models, learning packages, and diagnostic testing?

CRITERION-REFERENCED evaluation gives educators information about a student's achievement of a standard or objective established by the school and/or by the student.

State driver licensing tests are common examples of criterion-referenced measurement. The person taking the test must meet a predetermined standard, such as having a minimum number of errors on a written test, displaying a number of driving skills under varying conditions, and demonstrating practical knowledge of the rules of the road.

It makes no difference how the person ranks in terms of others who have taken the test either at the point he or she takes it or at any previous or later time. If the person meets the criterion, he or she receives a license.

An adequate criterion-referenced model must assist in the process of delineating, obtaining, and providing useful information for judging decision and accountability alternatives. Such an evaluation also provides information about the strengths and the weaknesses of alternative strategies and designs which were developed to achieve agreed-upon objectives.

The Model Schools Project, among other things, focused on curriculum content (both required and optional), the methods of teaching and learning (and where learning occurred), and student evaluation. Using a variety of questionnaires, the Udinsky-Keefe-Housden team sought to determine what program characteristics were being implemented by the schools. For example, one item asked teachers in various subject areas how often students were required to attend large-group presentations each week.

Among the other 19 items, teachers and students were asked to indicate the effectiveness of instructional assistants, clerical assistants, and general aides. In the area of large-group presentations, participants were asked about the use of demonstrations, debates, panels, films, and tapes. To evaluate small-group discussions, respondents were queried as to the various roles students played, including those of group leaders, recorders, observers, and consultants. Teachers and students reacted to the quality of learning packages, contracts, guides, and prescriptions, telling what they thought of the variation of activities each included.

Teacher and student responses to these items were separately computed, and profiles were developed for each

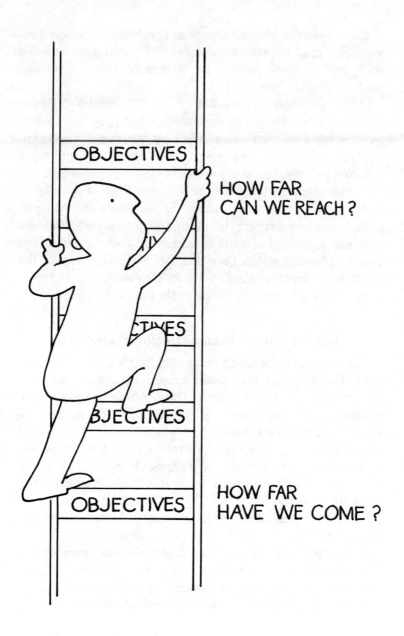

OBJECTIVES

HOW FAR
CAN WE REACH?

CTIVES

BJECTIVES

OBJECTIVES

HOW FAR
HAVE WE COME?

of these selected characteristics of the Model Schools Project. This criterion-referenced form of evaluation enabled each school to measure its progress toward specified goals and objectives.

Using a variety of questionnaires, the Udinsky, Keefe, Housden team sought to determine what program characteristics were being implemented by various schools. For example, teachers were asked how often students were required to attend large-group presentations each week.

These characteristics ultimately provided a profile of that school's curriculum model. These kinds of data permitted the researchers to compare the school's model with the extent of teacher-role change and to assess the degree of relationship between the two. The use of the traditional, norm-referenced types of evaluative materials would have been totally inadequate for this purpose.

Evaluation of Instructional Materials

The increasing growth of individualized learning systems has inspired the development of many forms of learning packages and guides. These range from the computer-assisted complexity of Individually Prescribed Instruction (IPI) and Planned Learning According to Needs (the teaching-learning units of Project PLAN as developed by the American Institute of Research) on the one hand, to the more conventional Learning Activity Packages and UNIPAC's on the other.

The Model called for an individualized learning system based upon a highly flexible time arrangement and a wide-ranging use of multiple materials and procedures. The student was given substantial responsibility for planning and carrying out an organized program of studies, with the assistance of teachers and paraprofessionals. The student's progress was determined primarily in terms of those plans. (Of course, individualized learning did not necessarily mean one teacher with one student. There were times when learning was individualized by clustering students into relatively large groups.)

The MSP Model for organizing individualized learning systems called for accommodating variations in students' styles and levels of learning, encouraging a wide variety of instructional materials and utilizing the basic instructional modes of large group, small group, tutorial, supervised study, and independent study.

The basic structure of individualized learning in the Model Schools was that of the learning package or unit. The curriculum of these learning units was designed for continuous progress through individualized pacing.

In many of the Model Schools, a unit of work was operationally defined as a segment of learning materials requiring the average student one or two weeks to complete. Resource materials were developed as a part of these units. The materials consisted of books, audiovisuals, charts and maps, tapes, films, models, teacher-prepared materials, projects, community activities, and work-experience alternatives. Students were able to work through a sequence of learning prescriptions at their own pace and level of difficulty, culminating in a test upon completion of the sequence.

Eventually, criterion-referenced evaluative models were organized to assess both the effectiveness and the implementation of this aspect of individualization.

A checklist was developed for students to critique each learning package or unit. The purpose was not to evaluate the subject matter content of the given unit but rather to determine its effectiveness in enabling the students to learn the curricular concepts contained therein. The six areas of a package to be evaluated were (1) format and directions, (2) concept focus, (3) behavioral objectives, (4) activities, methodologies, and resources, (5) quest— suggestions for breadth and depth work, and (6) evaluation devices. The evaluator was asked to indicate on a three-point scale the acceptability of each area.

The criterion-referenced evaluation for individualized instructional materials, as developed by Udinsky-Keefe-Housden, led to the identification of a number of successful guidelines for the development of sound packages. These included:

1. With regard to the instructional package format, it was found that it should be clear and uniform to avoid student confusion. At the same time there must be enough variety and creativity in the learning activities to obviate boredom.

2. There should be just one objective per learning package, and that objective should be stated simply and concisely. Component ideas, if any, had to be within the scope of the main idea and be appropriately sequenced.

3. The objective should be stated as a definite, observable behavior with appropriate, specific performance criteria included. All requisite conditions should be delineated within component ideas. The learning task should not be mere subject matter, and the objectives should frequently call for activities using the higher levels of Bloom's taxonomies.

4. Learning activities should contain some clearly specified alternatives or options to provide for the varying learning styles of youth.

5. Paper-and-pencil tests should be criterion-referenced rather than norm-referenced.

The obvious conclusion is that if one of the goals of a school is to produce individualized learning materials, then their quality must be assessed according to criterion-referenced evaluative standards. A school must be able to determine what procedures, methodologies, activities, and resources most effectively aid student growth, the Udinsky-Keefe-Housden study showed.

Diagnostic Testing of Students

Upon entering a program of individualized instruction, the student brings different backgrounds, interests, aptitudes, levels of achievement, and readiness for the various areas of learning. The whole concept of diagnosis implies that teachers, acting as facilitators or teacher-advisers, place every student at an appropriate entry level, that is, at that point in each learning sequence where the student displays the optimum aptitude, achievement, and readiness. A certain amount of this diagnosis can be and must be done orally, ascertaining what background the student has in a given subject area. Naturally, paper-and-pencil tests may help in this placement process.

Since the Model Schools Project called for the curriculum to be individualized in nine areas of learning—language arts, social studies, foreign languages, mathematics, science, fine arts, practical arts, physical education, and religion (in parochial schools)—a concerted effort was made in the early stages of the Project to develop criterion-referenced diagnostic instruments that would allow for proper placement of each student in each curricular area. During the five-year implementation schedule of the Model, schools began to develop measurements based on their own students' goals and objectives. Tests were used more and more, not so much to rate students, but to place them appropriately in the sequences. Commercially produced tests, used in the interim, were increasingly replaced by locally devised ones.

When a student entered a Model school, school personnel needed to know whether he or she should start at the beginning of the social studies or mathematics sequences or whether in fact the student had completed a part or a substantial majority of the work of those sequences. Instrumentation that keyed test items to individual student behaviors made this a practical reality.

As schools developed more sophisticated programs, they also developed diagnostic tests for major subdivisions of sequences. It was not enough to know that students could meet the major objectives of the ninth grade English sequence; rather, it was more important to know how they would do on such sub-areas as English communication skills, a knowledge of basic literature, their grasp of the principles of U.S. history, their knowledge of secretarial practice, their skills in basketball or volleyball, etc. At the close of five years in the Project, most schools did not yet have a full battery of tests for all subdivisions of all their learning sequences. Several schools, however, did have highly sophisticated instrumentation which had been statistically validated for content validity and reliability.

Content validity was established in many MSP schools by using the following systematic method:

- Required concepts and skills for the learning sequence or appropriate subdivision were developed.
- Behavioral objectives for each of the concepts or skills were specified.
- Test items (or item forms) were constructed for each objective. Items were selected from the content so that the test contained items in proper proportion to the importance of the subject matter or skills.

An example of the criterion-based measures used by Edgewood Junior High School in Mounds View, Minn., is shown in Table 1. At the beginning of the 1973-74 school year, several behavioral objectives were established to de-

40

Example of a Test Outline to Achieve Taxonomical Balance

Unit 1, Algebra I—Using Letters for Numbers

Objective	Taxonomy Classification Cognitive or Affective	Percentage Weight of Objective	Number of Test Items Used	Actual Percent of Total Items
1. Learning the meaning of terms.	Knowledge (cognitive)	20%	10	20%
2. Rules of using zero, parenthesis, exponents, like and unlike terms.	Knowledge (cognitive)	10%	6	12%
3. Recognize illustrations of the commutative principle.	Knowledge (cognitive)	5%	2	4%
4. The use of letters to stand for numbers.	Knowledge (cognitive)	5%	2	4%
5. Translate math symbols into verbal symbols & vice-versa.	Comprehension (cognitive)	20%	9	18%
6. Add, subtract, multiply and divide literal numbers.	Application (cognitive)	20%	12	24%
7. Evaluate and Substitute in algebraic expressions and formulas.	Application (cognitive)	10%	5	10%
8. Recognize the relationships among these ideas.	Analysis (cognitive)	5%	2	4%
9. Recognize the value of these concepts in daily living.	Attending (affective)	5%	2	4%
Totals	8 Cognitive 1 Affective	100%	50	100%

termine the success of the social science curriculum. Also developed were a means of measuring the attainment of the objectives and the criteria by which their attainment would be assessed.

TABLE 1
1973-1974 BEHAVIORAL OBJECTIVES

INTRODUCTION:

At the beginning of the 1973-74 school year several behavioral objectives were established to determine the success of the social science curriculum. Along with these objectives a means of measuring and the criteria used to determine whether the objectives were met had been set up.

The objectives, measurements, and criteria to be used are as follows:

Behavioral Objectives	As Measured By	Using the Following Criteria
1. Students will become self-motivated learners in social science.	The number of students who move from one curriculum level to another.	An average increase of one curriculum level per student per year.
2. Students will develop social skills in map reading, cartoon interpretation, graphs, tables, and charts as covered in the skills level curriculum.	A. The Social Sc. sub-test of SRA Achievement scores. B. The number of 7th grade students finishing S level.	A. The median score will be 7.9 or greater. B. At the end of Grade 7 = 85%
3. A. Students' attitudes toward social science activities will be positive.	Social Science Attitude Inventory	Student responses will be within 10% of department criteria.
B. Students will have a feeling of self-worth and value as persons through success.	Social Science Attitude Inventory	Student responses will be within 10% of department criteria.
C. Students will respect and develop concerns for the life styles and values of others.	Social Science Attitude Inventory	Student responses will be within 10% of department criteria.
4. Students will develop effective communication skills in speaking, listening, and interacting.	Small group and classroom checklist.	Student responses will meet the criteria established.

What We Learned

At the start of the Project, the schools encountered a serious shortage of criterion-referenced, diagnostic learning materials as well as a shortage of criterion-referenced tests for use in determining pupil growth and placement on continuums of learning sequences. As the five years of the Model passed, considerable progress was made in these areas. (Some of the school's results are reported in Chapter 5.) Nonetheless, there is much more to be done. The most significant progress in the development and application of criterion-referenced evaluation models will take place in the years to come.

Chapter 5 discusses progress toward the prescribed Model among participating schools. After all, progress toward the Model with improved learning conditions and learning outcomes is what the Project was all about.

Suggested Activities

1. Review a secondary school program which is attempting to diagnose student learning needs prior to prescribing specific learning experiences. Analyze the type of diagnostic instrument being used. Is criterion-referenced evaluation part of the diagnostic procedure?

2. Apply the content validity standard for criterion-referenced testing discussed in this chapter in the construction of an actual diagnostic test.

3. Obtain several examples of commercially or teacher-designed-and-developed learning packages or guides. Compare their construction and content to the criterion-referenced guidelines described in this chapter. How do they provide for different student learning styles and interests? How are multiple levels of cognitive thinking and affective behavior encouraged on the part of students?

5

Progress Toward the Model in MSP Schools

Don't all schools, whether they are innovative or conventional, have a model that constitutes the basis of their evaluation? Traditionally, the process of evaluation has been used as a culminating exercise to measure the success or failure of a final product. Recently, however, evaluation has gained a new sense of purpose with the advent of process or formative evaluation. Both standardized and locally developed measurement devices were used in the Model Schools Project by which schools assessed their growth and change.

R ALPH W. TYLER IN 1969 commented that there are two general stages experts go through in the assessment of educational innovations. The first stage is determining whether or not an institution is actually following the plan or model. In this context, the point is the degree administrators, teachers, and students are moving in a prearranged direction. Tyler's second stage of evaluation is determining some of the elements by which one might ascertain if a school is actually implementing the model it purports to be implementing.

44

Conventional Schools and Their Models

Conventional schools have guidelines on which their organization and direction are based. Their model can be traced to the regulations and recommendations of state departments of education, regional accrediting associations, universities, and local community needs. Additionally, a given school might well have an explicitly stated philosophy upon which its model is based.

One aspect of the model which has dominated conventional school evaluation for many decades is university admissions requirements. Unfortunately, conventional schools superimpose such a model upon unnecessarily large numbers of students regardless of their needs. Throughout this century, schools have evaluated their effectiveness by the success of their students in gaining admission to a variety of universities and the grade point averages that they maintain. Consequently, follow-up studies of graduates are made each year they are in college. Such an evaluation gives limited evidence of the actual quality of a high school program.

This model of evaluation is now being challenged. An increasing number of universities and colleges have established alternative kinds of criteria for admission. More and more, advanced placement courses are being offered on high school campuses. Furthermore, students are challenging course work offered in the freshman and sophomore years of universities and colleges. Pressure from certain socioeconomic and cultural minorities in the United States as well as declining enrollments and the problems of survival during the past few years have forced many universities and colleges to open their doors to students who were not previously admissible.

However, many students are not interested in attending college and want vocational and recreational type education. Despite this increase in pressure upon high schools to have programs for their many non-college oriented students, there has been little change in the evaluation model followed by most secondary schools. Many communities and conventional schools prefer this kind of simplistic evaluation. These criteria demand little of schools since the key factor to college success, as reported in numerous research studies, is the socioeconomic origin of the student, not the secondary school which he attended.

Another major component in models followed by most conventional schools is regional accreditation. This accrediting process can assist a staff analyze its diverse educational programs. In recent years, several of the regional accrediting associations have encouraged secondary schools in their movement toward individualization. Tragically, such encouragement has not produced significant change in the majority of the nation's secondary schools.

The Classic Model

Educational research has traditionally been planned, conducted, and summarized through the following classic model:

1. Pre-defining the nature of the program.
2. Inserting the program into an existing educational institution.
3. Measuring the results of the program against the original plan or model.
4. Contrasting the experimental treatment with the traditional or some other ongoing treatment which is assumed to have consistent and reliable dimensions.

One of the primary weaknesses of this classic model of research or curriculum evaluation is that it assumes program development and instructional methodology have been carried out with 100 percent consistency by all teachers and that all participating students have responded to it in a consistent manner. This is not often the case in real school settings. It is usually much easier to change titles or to change vocabulary than it is to change school personnel, curriculum, and goals.

The MSP Model

Consequently, the directors of the Model Schools Project felt it essential to measure progress *toward* the Model in each of the participating schools. The danger is, when moving into the stage of product or summative evaluation, one may be measuring a traditional program masquerading under an innovative title.

The evaluation design of an innovative program must be sensitive and responsive to the initial definition of the project as well as the on-going re-definition and modification that takes place as members implement program goals. Such evaluation provides information about the strengths and weaknesses of the strategy during the implementation. It asks and answers the question, "Are the procedures working properly?"

The formative or process evaluation utilized in the Model Schools Project was similar to the methods used by state or regional accrediting associations, but stated goals and measures were different. The basic aim was not to compare one school with another but rather for a given school to compare its progress toward the goals that it had previously defined and accepted. In the Model Schools Project, the Project staff as well as each school asked itself what progress it had made toward the objectives of the Project.

Annual progress-of-change reports were compiled by each of the high schools, local surveys were made to analyze the change process, the concept of teacher-role change was reviewed as suggested in the Udinsky-Keefe-Housden and O'Brien studies, certain aspects of the Metfessel evaluation model were applied, and use was made of student-administered self-tests as a part of student progress through various learning units. These became elements in assisting each school's assessment of its progress toward the Model as well as progress toward its own specific objectives.

Model Schools Project Annual Reports

Formally initiated in September 1969, the Model Schools Project collected data on the entire change process and compared these data on a yearly longitudinal basis. Data first collected in November 1970 to assess the 1969-70 school year were collected each year thereafter through the spring of 1974. The purpose of collecting the data was not only to monitor the progress of the schools, but also to determine what aspects of schools were more difficult to change and why.

All schools in the Project were asked to estimate progress in each aspect of the Model. The data were consolidated by averaging percentage information provided by the schools in answer to such directives as the following:

—Indicate how much time the principal spends on each of the following aspects of his job in hours per week: improvement of instruction _____; school management _____; other (specify) _____. (This information was subsequently changed to percentages of time.)

—Give total hours of clerical assistance provided each week per teacher _____. (These data were changed to percentages of the Model goal of 10 hours per week per teacher.)

—Number of teachers with each of the following types of offices: private _____; semi-private (in a room with others) _____; in a room with other teachers with no visual barriers _____. (This was eventually reported for each response as percentages of the total teaching staff.)

—How many pupils regularly receive other than A, B, C, D, or F grades? _____. How many pupils regularly receive reports of special projects completed? _____.

Findings from the annual reports were published in the May issues of the *NASSP Bulletin* from 1971 to 1974. The 1971 annual report contained key data on the progress of change toward the Model.

The schools were divided into three categories:

(1) seven schools with which the Project staff worked most closely and which were given some funds for teacher training and development;

(2) another seven schools that received some personal visits and special training from the Project staff;

(3) the balance of the schools in the Project—those experiencing few personal contacts with the Project staff, most communication taking place by telephone and letter, plus a group of newly opened schools.

Tables 1, 2, and 3 on the following pages show the average percentage of progress among the schools in each of 18 aspects of the Model. Average percentages are given for each of the three categories, ranging from 0 (no progress) to 100 percent (complete achievement) of that particular aspect of the Model. Table 1 groups six aspects of the MSP that were *most difficult* for schools to change. Table 3 groups six aspects of the MSP where the percentages of achievement were largest; therefore, these aspects were *easiest* to change. Table 2 lists six aspects of medium difficulty between the two extremes.

Most Difficult To Change

Column I in Table 1 refers to the Model's objective of a teacher-pupil ratio of 1 to 35 (total number of teachers, not counting special teachers, counselors, or assistant principals, divided into the total number of pupils). This high ratio was considered essential if the appropriate numbers of aides were to be employed within existing budgets. Without adequate staff differentiation, the lower adult-pupil ratio would not be realized.

Progress was slow toward this goal, with schools in Category 1 adding only four pupils per teacher during the first year of the Model. On the average, schools traveled only 14 percent of the way toward full implementation of this goal. However, one school in Category 1 achieved 94 percent of this objective. Slow progress toward this objective indicated teacher resistance to reducing the size of the certificated faculty. The tradition of the teacher serving as a clerk, bookkeeper, compiler of records, and babysitter apparently is difficult to change.

Column II portrays the extent to which MSP schools eliminated the traditional A, B, C, D, F letter grades and moved to more descriptive and comprehensive methods of reporting student progress. The average extent of implementation in Category 1 schools was 31 percent, with two schools reporting 100 percent fulfillment. Category 2 showed a very low average (0.1 percent) with the best school only 0.4 percent along the way, having eliminated letter grades in only one course. Category 3 averaged 17 percent accomplishment, with one school reporting 100 percent by the end of the first year of the Project.

Column III refers to schools that made it possible for students to complete subjects in time spans other than quarters, semesters, and/or years. The figures indicate that schools in Category 1 progressed an average of 47 percent of the way toward full implementation of the goal of continuous progress, with two schools reporting 100 percent. Those schools in Category 2 averaged 17 percent, while those in Category 3 reported a low 12 percent attainment of this goal.

Column IV—Parts A, B, and C—shows the extent to which the schools achieved the differentiated staff that the MSP required. The percentages indicate more progress than in changing the teacher-pupil ratio (Column I), illustrating a willingness to employ paraprofessionals at added cost to the school districts.

Column IV-A represents the progress schools made in employing general aides, based on the Model's goal of five hours per week of such aide service per teacher. Category 1 averaged 26 percent; Category 2, 26 percent; and Category 3, 19 percent. Only one school reported 100 percent fulfillment.

Column IV-B shows the progress the schools made in employing clerical assistants, based on 10 hours a week per teacher. Category 1 averaged 37 percent; Category 2, 30 percent; and Category 3, 10 percent.

Column IV-C indicates the progress the schools made in employing instructional assistants at the 20-hours-per-week-per-teacher ratio established by the Model. Category 1 averages 34 percent; Category 2, 36 percent; and Category 3, 17 percent. Once again, only one school reported 100 percent attainment.

Column V shows the degree to which the schools made provisions for private or semi-private office facilities for each teacher. Category 1 showed a low average of 8 percent implementation of this objective, while Categories 2 and 3 reported a 42 percent and 47 percent achievement, respectively.

Inadequate space was usually cited as the reason for not providing offices and work spaces for teachers. Yet, teachers can hardly be expected to function as professionals and

TABLE 1

Aspects of the Model Which Were Most Difficult To Implement
1969-70 School Year

Category of Schools	Average Percent of Change from 0% to 100% Selected Aspects of the NASSP Model for Schools							
	I	II	III	IV Differentiate Staff			V	VI
				A	B	C		
	Increase Teacher-Pupil Ratio (from present to 1:35)	Use More Comprehensive Reporting System in Place of A, B, C, D, F	Make Possible That All Pupils May Complete Subjects in Time Spans Other Than Quarters, Semesters, Years	Employ General Aides (5 hours per week per teacher)	Employ Clerical Assistants (10 hours per week per teacher)	Employ Instructional Assistants (20 hours per week per teacher)	Provide Each Teacher with Private or Semi-private Office	Evaluative Pupil Progress: Completion of Special Projects
1	14	31	47	26	37	34	8	24
2	18	1	17	26	30	36	42	61
3	10	17	12	19	10	17	47	23

relate to pupils as teacher-advisers unless they have privacy. The greatest deterrent to the achievement of this goal may have been the refusal of the schools to reallocate space—to break the traditional grip of some persons and departments on the use of certain space. A number of the schools also persisted in the wasteful and costly practice of having teachers work in classrooms that were needlessly devoid of pupils for a time.

Column VI refers to evaluation of pupil progress. The figures were based on completion of projects by the students. The Model placed high priority on appraising, recording, and describing these projects as a more complete report to parents of student progress. The conventional school conceals such information in a single letter grade. Category 1 averaged 24 percent with one school reporting 100 percent. Category 2 averaged 61 percent, with three schools showing 100 percent; and Category 3 averaged 23 percent, with three schools at the 100 percent achievement level.

Making it possible and desirable for pupils to work on special projects, to develop particular interests, or to pursue areas in depth beyond the normal classroom seems to be difficult. Yet, it is in this kind of activity that the unique personality of each pupil is discovered and encouraged as he or she goes beyond the minimum requirements expected of everyone. Instruction can hardly be individualized until this practice is possible for all pupils. Lack of teacher time or interest may have been a contributing factor which militated against progress in this area.

Somewhat Less Difficult To Change

Table 2 presents the middle six characteristics of the Model. These six items were easier to change than the first six but not as easy as those covered in Table 3. Although the Table 2 average percentages of change were higher than the Table 1 averages—when considered together for the total group—they were in the range of from about one-half to two-thirds of the distance from 0 to 100 percent achievement of the Model.

Column VII of this table represents the degree to which provision was made, if not for offices, at least for special rooms in which teachers could work. Such facilities were temporary, a transitional step towards private or semi-private office space. Category 1 averaged 63 percent implementation with one school reporting 100 percent. Category 2 averaged 47 percent and also had one school with 100 percent; Category 3 averaged 47 percent and showed three schools with 100 percent. This objective may be somewhat easier to achieve than providing private offices for teachers, since larger space (typically vacant classrooms) can frequently be converted into departmental offices or workrooms. Such spaces became available in schools trying to achieve the Model because the latter required less building space than the conventional school as a result of its more efficient space utilization.

TABLE 2
Aspects of the 'Model of Medium Difficulty for the Schools To Change
1969-70 School Year

Category of Schools	Percent of Change from 0% to 100% in Selected Aspects of the NASSP Model for Schools					
	VII Provide (at least) Special Rooms for Teachers to Work In (merely a transitional step)	VIII Make Available Continuous Progress Arrangements for Pupils	IX Teacher-Advisers Schedule Pupils' Independent Study	X Evaluate Pupil Progress: Record Completion of Segments in the Required Learning Sequences in the Various Subject Areas	XI Pupils Spend 4 hours per week in Motivational Presentations (larger than classroom groups)	XII Teachers Provide Motivational Presentations (larger than classroom groups)
1	63	60	65	60	50	34
2	47	34	63	78	50	65
3	47	63	56	53	92	100

Column VIII shows the extent to which the continuous progress arrangements were available for all pupils. The Model's goal was 100 percent availability in all subjects. Category 1 averaged 60 percent achievement, with four schools indicating 100 percent attainment. Category 2 dipped to a 34 percent level, with but one school at 100 percent; Category 3 averaged 63 percent, with again just one school at 100 percent.

54

A notable inconsistency exists between Column VIII in this table and Column III in Table 1, both dealing with the concept of arranging curriculum on a sequential basis. Considerably more than half of the schools arranged a continuous progress curriculum, but less than one-fifth of them, except for the schools in Category 1 (47 percent), permitted pupils to complete a subject at any time. Credit for completing work had to be at the end of a quarter, semester, or year.

In reality, there can be no continuous progress based on concepts of time. The arrangement of the curriculum in a sequential format is a necessary prelude, but it must be followed by the abandonment of time as the basis for credit if true individualization is provided.

Column IX shows the extent to which teacher-advisers helped students schedule their independent study time. Category 1 averaged a 65 percent attainment; Category 2, 63 percent; and Category 3, 56 percent. Category 3 reported three schools at the 100 percent level while the other two categories had two each. Interestingly, a great majority of the schools had implemented the teacher-adviser role, as shown in Table 3, Column XVI. However, the fact that considerably fewer of the schools gave the teacher-adviser a major responsibility for working with the pupils' programs indicates *it is easier to change the structure of a school than it is to change what people do*. The first is superficial; the latter is basic.

Column X refers to the schools' evaluation of pupil progress with respect to their completion of segments in the required learning sequences. Category 1 averaged 60 percent; Category 2, 78 percent; and Category 3, 56 percent. Five schools in Category 3 reported 100 percent fulfillment whereas the other two categories reported two schools each at the 100 percent level.

The contrast between these data and the findings reported in Table 1, Columns II and VI, should be noted. Apparently it is much easier to keep track of each pupil's progress in completing learning packages, chapters, units, or other segments in a required learning sequence than it is to evaluate special projects or *especially* to get rid of grading on A, B, C, D, and F basis.

Column XI shows the degree to which schools implement the Model's goal of pupils spending four hours per week in large-group motivational presentations. Categories 1 and 2 averaged 50 percent whereas Category 3 had 92 percent. Five schools in the last group reported 100 percent fulfillment of the Model's goal while Categories 1 and 2 reported two and one school, respectively, at this level.

Column XII, by contrast, shows the degree of implementation of large-group motivational presentations. The Model proposed two hours per week per teacher. Category 1 showed a 34 percent average; Category 2, 65 percent; and Category 3 showed an unprecedented 100 percent fulfillment by all schools in this group. Category 1 had but one school at this level, while Category 2 reported two at 100 percent.

Large-group presentations have been characteristic of team-teaching designs for many years. They have not, however, been motivationally oriented. To arrange such presentations for 30 minutes a week in each of eight subject areas (or nine in parochial schools, including religion) demands a reorganization of the entire school schedule. Apparently the majority of schools found such a program easy to schedule. Of course, the question remains, how motivational were these sessions?

Least Difficult To Change

Finally, we come to the six aspects of the Model that principals found easiest to change. The percentages in Table 3 show achievement of nearly three-fourths of each of the six goals of the Model. For example, the least difficult change was the scheduling of pupils into smaller than classroom-size groups for motivational discussions, summarized in Column XVIII.

Column XIII of Table 3 shows the extent to which teachers became involved in the development of learning packages. Category 1 averaged 77 percent; Category 2, 76 percent; and Category 3, 59 percent. Category 1 reported three schools at the 100 percent level, while the other two categories reported two each at 100 percent. Junior high school teachers in one Category 1 school produced more than 1,600 packages for their continuous progress program.

Generally speaking, it was relatively easy to get teachers to prepare curriculum packages because of accessible workshops at nearby universities and in the school districts themselves. Although this achievement said little about the quality of such packages, the development signified a good deal of constuctive teacher activity in an appropriate direction.

Column XIV shows the amount of teacher involvement with small group motivational discussions (defined as taking place in smaller than regular class-size groups), a percentage based on the Model's goal of eight hours per week in this activity. Category 1 averaged 60 percent; Category 2, 78 percent; and Category 3, 81 percent. Category 1 reported one school at 100 percent fulfillment, Category 2 had three, and Category 3 reported five. Considerable progress was made toward the organization of small group motivational discussions.

Column XV, Parts A through I, indicate the extent to which all pupils had systematic, continuous contacts with all eight basic curriculum areas (religion being the ninth area in parochial schools). Category 1 schools averaged at or above the 75 percent level of achievement in English, mathematics, social studies, science, health and physical education, and the practical arts, but dropped off to a 61 percent level for fine arts and a low 48 percent in the area of cultures of foreign countries.

Category of Schools	Average Percent of Change from 0% to 100% in Selected Aspects of the NASSP Model for Schools													
	XIII	XIV	XV									XVI	XVII	XVIII
			Pupils Have Systematic, Continuous Contacts with All Curriculum Areas											
			A	B	C	D	E	F	G	H	I			
	Teachers Make Learning Packages	Teachers Meet Pupils for Motivational Discussions (smaller than classroom-size groups)	Fine Arts	Other Cultures (For. Lang.)	Practical Arts	Science	Mathematics	Social Studies	Health, Fitness, Recreation (PE)	English	Religion (Cath.)	Create the Teacher-Adviser Role	Principal Spends 3/4 of His Time on Improving Instruction	Pupils Spend Time in Motivational Discussions (in smaller than classroom-size groups)
1	77	60	61	48	75	75	77	85	83	96	100	91	74	60
2	76	78	39	57	66	66	69	74	87	100	100	72	83	100
3	59	81	56	59	71	71	77	86	80	97	97	66	72	100

The Category 2 schools averaged a 74 percent level or higher in three of these areas—English, health and physical education, and social studies; however, they were lower than Category 1 in all other areas except in the study of foreign cultures.

Category 3 schools showed less variance in their averages, ranging from a 97 percent in English to a 56 percent in fine arts. Continuous contact in the fine arts was the most difficult to implement, followed closely by a study of other cultures.

These curricular findings are generally consistent with school practices found in the past. Schools have long required continuous contact in the subjects of English, mathematics, social studies, and physical education. However, the MSP schools broadened continuous contact to include science and the practical arts in many cases. If all the basic areas of human learning are to be given equal consideration, such contacts must be expanded further to include cultures of foreign countries and the fine arts. The concept of curriculum equality appears to have gained some momentum in the Model schools.

Column XVI reports the degree to which teachers were functioning in a daily teacher-adviser role for a group of 30-35 students. Category 1 averaged 91 percent, with four schools reporting a 100 percent achievement. Categories 2 and 3 averaged 75 percent and 66 percent, respectively, each reporting two schools at the 100 percent level.

Structural changes, such as a teacher's being assigned to 30 students as an adviser, are easily arranged. The question still is what are teachers doing in this role that is uniquely different from the old homeroom adviser role? Unless they confer regularly with individual pupils and rearrange programs and schedules for each as needed, individualized instruction will not become a reality. (Table 2, Column IX lends insight into the slowness with which the teacher-adviser role was used in aiding students with scheduling independent study time.)

Column XVII shows the extent to which principals were devoting at least 75 percent of their time to improving instruction. Category 1 averaged 75 percent; Category 2, 83 percent; and Category 3, 72 percent. By reorganizing patterns of responsibility, principals were able to release themselves for instructional leadership.

Column XVIII corroborates the findings of Column XIV with respect to the implementation of small-group discussions. Such discussions may have proven comparatively easy to achieve because of their appeal to both teachers and pupils.

The following list summarizes the MSP schools' implementation of the various aspects of the Model. Although this rank order is for the first year of the evaluation study, there was little change during the following four years. The 18 selected aspects are listed in rank order from most difficult to least difficult with their average percentage of change across all the schools of the Project.

1. Increase teacher-pupil ratio (from 1968 ratios to that of one teacher for every 35 students)—14 percent.

2. Use more comprehensive grade reporting system in place of A, B, C, D, F—16 percent.

3. Make possible for all pupils to complete subjects in time spans other than quarters, semesters, years—25 percent.

4. Employ a differential staff (instructional, clerical, and general aides according to Model prescriptions)—26 percent.

5. Provide each teacher with private or semi-private office—32 percent.

6. Provide for the evaluation of pupil special projects—36 percent.

7. Provide special teacher workrooms as a transitional step to offices—52 percent.

8. Make available continuous progress arrangements for pupils—52 percent.

9. Reorganize staff assignments so that teacher-adviser schedule pupils' independent study—61 percent.

10. Record completion of segments in the required learning sequences of the various subject areas in evaluating pupil progress—64 percent.

11. Provide time for students to spend four hours per week in motivational presentations — 64 percent.

12. Provide large group motivational presentations — 66 percent.

13. Make learning packages — 71 percent.

14. Meet pupils for small group motivational discussions — 73 percent.

15. Provide pupils with systematic, continuous contacts with all eight or nine curriculum areas — 76 percent.

16. Establish a teacher-adviser role — 76 percent.

17. Redesign schedule to allow the principal to spend 3/4 of his time on improving instruction — 76 percent.

18. Schedule student time to allow pupils to spend time in small-group motivational discussions — 87 percent.

Although percentage data averaged across all schools provide only a crude estimate of the change process, the Project directors were able to detect broad trends and problems of a more serious nature by analyzing the data. For example, it became apparent in subsequent evaluations and annual reports that the initial categories established in the Project to classify schools did not discriminate well among those schools that showed a greater or lesser degree of change. Schools in Category 3 frequently showed as much or more change than schools in Category 1, which were receiving considerably more financial assistance and consultative help from the Project staff.

These data caused the Project staff to plan more extensive evaluation of individual schools by both external and internal researchers. It also became apparent that the various Model Schools should not be compared with one another but that each should be compared against its own baseline data

Impetus for change was frequently the result of a strong supervisory-management team, highly interested and informed district office persons, or unusually strong commitment by teachers. Such variables often had a more significant impact on the change which occurred than did financial assistance or consultative help from the Project staff. The Project seemed to serve more as a catalyst than a source of direct aid to Category 3 schools.

The chapter which follows provides additional research data on progress made toward implementation of the Model. It consists of local school surveys, analysis of the teacher's role in the Model Schools Project, and a summary of other studies.

Suggested Activities

1. Survey and review the literature describing the methods and uses of *process* (formative) and *product* (summative) evaluation. Briefly design an evaluative model which employs both process and product evaluation components.

2. Review some of the means utilized among the Model Schools to measure progress toward the Model. Design a limited evaluation model based on some of the findings of this Project.

3. Apply the DPIE format to your school. Determine how much diagnosis, prescription, implementation, and evaluation has taken place and what the impact has been on student growth.

6

Additional Research Data

What kinds of worthwhile informal surveys were made of the MSP by participating schools? In particular, what kind of detailed analysis was made of the changed role of the teacher under the Model? An exhaustive study was made of Bishop Carroll High School in Canada, the school that best exemplified all aspects of the MSP. Finally, all of the schools continued their use of norm-based testing. What were some of the findings from these various evaluative devices?

To FURTHER DETERMINE progress toward the Model, many individual schools developed survey instruments and administered them annually to the professional staff, paraprofessional assistants, students, and parents. These survey instruments usually employed a Likert-type format and reported responses in percentages. Several schools used a survey in which teachers, aides, and students were asked to evaluate the school's learning environment, large-group presentations, small-group discussions, independent or self-directed study, the teacher adviser role, and differentiated staffing.

The section of one questionnaire administered by a school in the Project focused on learning environment and asked respondents whether students had the same or more or less opportunity to engage in the following types of activities:

—To get individual help from teachers

—To make friends with many other students

—To learn to think for themselves

—To work independently without direct teacher supervision

—To use a variety of printed materials besides textbooks

—To study topics in which they are personally interested

—To see the purposes for learning the subject matter

—To use the community for resources not available in the school.

Data from these surveys were used to determine the degree of implementation of the different concepts and to ascertain problems that needed special attention. For example, well over 80 percent of the respondents at one school indicated that students had the same or better opportunities for an effective learning environment under the Model. They expressed an even higher percentage of support for concepts like independent study, the teacher-adviser role, and differentiated staffing.

The respondents indicated problems, however, with the concepts of large groups and small groups, suggesting that the modality of motivational presentation or discussion left something to be desired. When queried in person, students indicated that large-group and small-group sessions were not worthwhile unless the sessions were directly content-related.

Schools in the Project perceiving this problem gradually moved the focus of large groups and small groups toward more subject-related topics. Some schools, in addition, reduced the frequency of large groups and small groups. These modifications provide a good illustration of how formative evaluation can provide a feedback loop for "midcourse change" in innovative programs. Within the framework of the Model Schools Project this could happen, for schools were not locked into an arbitrary, inflexible system.

The Teacher's Role in the MSP

A major finding of both the Udinsky-Keefe-Housden (UKH) and O'Brien studies was the change of the teacher's role from the conventional dispenser of information to one of a director or facilitator of student learning.

To provide a schema for evaluation, the UKH study identified seven areas that best described the emerging new role of the teacher:

1. *Teacher-Adviser*. The teacher in the Model Schools Project assumed both the role of a director of learning and the role of an adviser to a group of 25-35 students. In the latter role, the teacher helped students in formulating their schedules, arranging their independent study time, evaluating their progress, etc. The teacher was also a special friend to advisees, ready to assist them with their ordinary school problems.

2. *Differentiated Staffing*. Teachers functioned as members of a team of professionals and paraprofessionals (instructional aides and clerks) in which different responsibilities were assumed and performed by each member according to his or her status and capabilities.

3. *Large-Group Presentation*. Teacher-planned presentations were (a) primarily motivational in nature but were also (b) informational, providing facts and ideas not readily available to students, and (c) directional, suggesting or assigning independent activities as further study to be done.

4. *Small-Group Discussion.* These were student-centered learning activities where pupils were to learn to communicate effectively, to listen to and respect the opinions of others, etc. In these discussions, teachers acted in a supportive and facilitative role.

5. *Independent Study.* Independent study was defined as those activities in which pupils engage when their teachers stop talking. It was that time spent by students, either alone or in groups, to complete the basic requirements of the program in each of the areas of human knowledge and to develop personal talents and interests. During student time for independent study, teachers assumed the role of consultant and director of learning strategies.

6. *Continuous Progress.* This concept was predicated on a nongraded curriculum and inter-age groupings, assuming that learning is the satisfactory accomplishment of a series of stated performance objectives irrespective of the time necessary for such completion. Continuous progress presumed that teachers would develop properly validated learning packages or guides and would assist students in their self-paced, self-directed learning experiences through diagnosis, prescription, and evaluation.

7. *Student Grading.* The Model Schools Project suggested that participating schools downplay conventional grading systems and emphasize more what pupils actually know and do. In preparing student progress reports, teachers were to indicate descriptively the nature of student achievement, the amount of progress a student had made along the continuum in that subject area, and the satisfactory completion (if any) of special projects.

An instrument was designed to assess the degree to which teachers as a group had progressed toward 100 percent implementation of these eight defined areas of change. (See Appendix B.) The extent of teacher-role change was reported within individual schools and across all schools of the Project.

The across-school data were presented in a cumulative form for each of the seven sub-areas of teacher role change, and a composite extent-of-teacher-role-change score, known as CETRC, was derived for teachers, students, and principals for all participating 29 schools.

Table 1 shows subscale and composite "extent-of-teacher-role-change" scores for both the UKH and O'Brien studies across all schools of the Project. All sub-scale areas showed improvement from 1971 to 1973 for principals,

TABLE 1
Comparison of Principal, Teacher, and Student
Extent of Teacher Role Change (ETRC), Subscale and Composite
Scores, Across Schools—UKH study (1971) and O'Brien study (1973)

Principals	UKH (N = 29)		O'Brien (N = 20)	
	Mean	Range	Mean	Range
Teacher-Adviser	4.43	0.0-9.0	5.70	0.0-8.7
Differentiated Staffing	5.54	2.0-9.0	6.13	4.7-8.0
Large-Group Presentation	4.94	0.0-8.0	5.44	0.0-8.4
Small-Group Discussion	6.07	2.0-8.5	6.47	3.0-9.0
Independent Study	5.29	2.3-8.7	6.06	3.3-8.3
Continuous Progress	5.19	1.0-8.5	6.30	4.0-8.0
Student Grading	3.73	0.0-8.5	5.83	1.7-8.8
Composite	4.79	2.3-8.0	5.97	3.4-7.8

Teachers	UKH (N = 29)		O'Brien (N = 20)	
	Mean	Range	Mean	Range
Teacher-Adviser	4.26	1.4-7.6	5.37	1.6-7.7
Differentiated Staffing	5.18	3.2-7.4	5.79	4.3-7.7
Large-Group Presentation	4.61	2.0-7.1	5.03	4.3-6.2
Small-Group Discussion	5.37	3.3-7.7	5.51	3.9-7.5
Independent Study	4.74	2.5-7.1	5.68	4.3-7.4
Continuous Progress	5.10	2.7-6.7	6.02	4.5-7.6
Student Grading	3.62	1.3-7.7	5.05	2.3-7.9
Composite	4.52	2.8-7.0	5.35	4.2-7.4

Students	UKH (N = 1435)		O'Brien (N = 956)	
	Mean	Range	Mean	Range
Teacher-Adviser	4.49	2.5-6.6	4.72	1.0-6.9
Differentiated Staffing	5.30	2.2-7.6	5.64	3.8-6.9
Large-Group Presentation	4.61	0.9-7.0	4.58	0.7-6.8
Small-Group Discussion	5.61	3.8-7.4	5.48	4.2-7.0
Independent Study	4.50	2.8-6.7	4.99	4.0-7.0
Continuous Progress	5.12	3.0-7.7	5.21	3.3-7.3
Student Grading	4.50	1.8-6.8	5.04	2.7-7.6
Composite	4.80	2.7-6.7	5.08	3.1-7.1

teachers, and students with the exception of the large group and small group sub-areas as evaluated by students. In both the latter cases, mean scores showed a slight downward trend, perhaps reflecting the ambiguity detected by local school surveys about these two areas of the Model.

Table 2 shows the rank order of principal, teacher, and student extent-of-teacher-role-change with subscale means, comparing the two studies. Small-group discussion achieved the highest level of implementation in both 1971 and 1973. Differentiated staffing, independent study, and continuous progress held somewhat comparable positions in both studies. The use of large-group presentations showed a downward trend and sounder student grading a marked uptrend by the fourth year of the Model.

Some tentative conclusions might be drawn from the data in these two studies. Teachers in the earlier evaluation saw administrative leadership as the prime contributing factor. In 1973, support had moved to the element of differentiated staffing.

It would appear that strong administrative leadership is needed in the early stages of innovation. As innovation flourishes, however, there is reason to believe that the staff will assume more responsibility for its own growth and change.

When the data on student, teacher, and principal perceptions are analyzed from a broader perspective, it is obvious that these three groups view the school in somewhat different fashions. Undoubtedly principals see the school from one viewpoint—a leadership one, perhaps even an unrealistic one. Although teachers and students tend to agree, teachers see the school from a middle position and may reflect the pressures of that situation. Students are less informed about the technical aspects of innovative strategy but do know what is happening to them.

Prominent among the features of the Model (and critical to an assessment of progress toward the Model) were the

TABLE 2
Comparative Rank Order of Principal, Teacher, j nd Student
ETRC Sub-scale Means, Across Schools—UKH (1971) and
O'Brien (1973) Studies.

Principals

	UKH			O'Brien	
1.	Small-Group Discussion	6.07	1.	Small-Group Discussion	6.47
2.	Differentiated Staffing	5.54	2.	Continuous Progress	6.30
3.	Independent Study	5.29	3.	Differentiated Staffing	6.13
4.	Continuous Progress	5.19	4.	Independent Study	6.06
5.	Large-Group Presentation	4.94	5.	Student Grading	5.83
6.	Teacher-Adviser	4.43	6.	Teacher Adviser	5.70
7.	Student Grading	3.73	7.	Large-Group Presentation	5.44

Teachers

	UKH			O'Brien	
1.	Small-Group Discussion	5.37	1.	Continuous Progress	6.02
2.	Differentiated Staffing	5.18	2.	Differentiated Staffing	5.79
3.	Continuous Progress	5.10	3.	Independent Study	5.68
4.	Independent Study	4.74	4.	Small-Group Discussion	5.51
5.	Large-Group Presentation	4.61	5.	Teacher-Adviser	5.37
6.	Teacher-Adviser	4.26	6.	Student Grading	5.05
7.	Student Grading	3.62	7.	Large-Group Presentation	5.03

Students

	UKH			O'Brien	
1.	Small-Group Discussion	5.61	1.	Differentiated Staffing	5.64
2.	Differentiated Staffing	5.30	2.	Small-Group Discussion	5.48
3.	Continuous Progress	5.12	3.	Continuous Progress	5.21
4.	Large-Group Presentation	4.61	4.	Student Grading	5.04
5.	Independent Study	4.50	5.	Independent Study	4.99
6.	Student Grading	4.50	6.	Teacher-Adviser	4.72
7.	Teacher-Adviser	4.49	7.	Large-Group Presentation	4.58

areas of large-group presentation and small-group discussion. It was important to design special instrumentation to evaluate the progress toward the use of such student groupings, to determine whether these methodologies were meeting the specifications of the Model, and to assess the quality of their application. In 1973, Neal W. Olsen and Robert Amenta, two doctoral students who were high school principals, developed scales to measure such progress.

69

Olsen identified major factors which influence and/or indicate the effectiveness of large-group presentations. He also specified various elements which might be included within each factor and whether they are positive or negative in their effect. In addition, he attached a point value to each of the elements to indicate its relative effectiveness with respect to the overall presentation.

To illustrate, the following are examples of two factors in the rating scale with some of their identified elements:

Factors	Elements
Methodology	Lecture
	Demonstration
	Panel discussion
	Question-Answer
	Media
	Etc.
Student reaction	Paying rapt attention
	Moderate positive attention
	Observing passively
	Negative attention

This scale provided a complicated, but authentic rating of any motivational large-group presentation.

In a similar vein, Amenta assessed the qualities of small-group instruction in the Project and developed an observation instrument. This scale lists the characteristics of an effective small group and provides a rating system to evaluate the quality of the discussion.

Scales such as those developed by Amenta and Olsen and individual schools emerged toward the conclusion of the Project. Consequently, there was little opportunity to utilize them on a wide scale. They should be of considerable help in the future as schools attempt to assess educational innovation.

Other Studies

An extensive study was conducted in one of the Model Schools under the title of "Performance as a Basis for Credit—An Evaluation Study of Secondary School Programs—An ESEA Title III Project." This study focused on the most prominent goals mentioned nationally by parents, school administrators, and teachers: 1) better attitudes toward school; 2) better self concept; 3) better attitudes toward self responsibility; 4) better attitudes toward learning and education. Among other national goals mentioned were improvement of basic skills and keeping students in school (attendance).

This study also included an assessment of the attitudes of parents toward Leo High School in Fort Wayne, Ind., and the attitudes of Leo High School graduates toward its program. The following selected conclusions are based upon the findings of the study;

- Although there is no evidence of attitude change overall in grades nine through 12, students in grade nine at Leo High School exhibited a positive change in attitude toward learning and education.

- Students attending grades 11 and 12 in Leo High School seemed to be more responsible.

- Students at Leo High School indicated a trend toward a more positive self, while the evidence showed the controlled school students in a negative direction of self concept.

- While Leo High School students (grade seven in 1973 and grade eight in 1974) scored slightly higher in reading achievement, there was no significant difference between scores made by both Leo and the controlled school.

- The trend from surveyed graduates seemed to support the Leo program when asked if their high school experience helped them since leaving school. This seems to counteract the parental attitudes toward the program and supports the student's attitude toward the school.

Norm-Based Evaluation Results

During 1974-75 Anne Scott and William Georgiades studied the cognitive achievement of students in five schools that had been reasonably successful in implementing many aspects of the Model. The School and College Ability Test (SCAT) and the Sequential Test of Educational Progress (STEP) were administered to a 20 percent random sample of tenth, eleventh, and twelfth grade students in each of the participating schools. These tests provided nationally-normed aptitudes and achievement scores that could be used for comparison purposes.

A detailed analysis of the results showed no significant differences between the aptitude means of Model Schools Project students and the national norms. (Had the Project staff skewed the selection process in identifying schools to participate in the program, the results could have been distorted. Schools were chosen with an effort to maintain a cosmopolitan, national type of representativeness.) Thus, the SCAT test results supported the representativeness of the Project schools.

Consequently, one can conclude that students enrolled in the Model Schools Project achieved at levels which were commensurate with their aptitudes and that they did not suffer in terms of cognitive achievement as a consequence of attending an MSP school. At the same time, they showed much affective gain in progressing towards disparate, individualized learning objectives.

Further, students in the Model Schools Project were consistently exposed to all eight or nine areas of human learning as contrasted with students in conventional schools who were taking no more than four or five subject areas each semester.

This chapter has been devoted to a discussion of the many ways in which progress toward the MSP Model was measured by schools participating in the Project. In addition to the studies reported, there were many smaller studies conducted by individual schools. What is of primary importance is not so much the technique, the means, or the precise evaluative processes which were used, but rather the measurement of progress toward the Model to which these schools had committed themselves. As discussed, every school has a model; each must be held accountable, in terms of its objectives, to implement that model.

The next chapter discusses the ways in which schools participating in the Model Schools Project attempted to measure their progress toward the Model through the use of time logs.

Suggested Activities

1. Organize a model to utilize both norm-based and criterion-referenced evaluation in your specialty subject field. Suggest ways in which such evaluative data can be communicated to both pupils and parents.

2. Develop an attitudinal scale to assess pupil and teacher attitudes toward the school program. Suggest ways in which such information might be utilized through discussion groups, etc., in assisting the school to strengthen its program.

7

Measuring the Use of Time

The diagnosis-prescription-implementation-evaluation cycle was a key ingredient in the "master plan" of the Model Schools Project. How did students, teachers, and the supervisory-management team reorganize and restructure the use of time during the school day? To measure the success of participating schools' ability to implement the DPIE cycle, a series of Time-Activities-Characteristic-Products Studies was conducted.

ONE OF THE GOALS OF THE Model Schools Project was to develop a high school program that would reflect the needs, the expectancies, and the desires of both its community and its student population. The realization that humans do not learn by semesters and that the pace of learning varies dramatically from person to person led to the development of a cycle which would recognize individual rates of learning. This came to be called the diagnosis-prescription-implementation-evaluation (DPIE) cycle.

During the diagnostic phase, it is important to find answers for each student to questions such as: Where is the student on a learning continuum? What is his or her background of experiences? What does he or she know and how does he or she learn? What are his or her attitudes? The gathering of this kind of information leads to a prescription or program individually designed for the student.

Undergirding the DPIE cycle is the need to rearrange substantially the six- or seven-period daily mode of the conventional school. How can teachers diagnose appropriately if they are teaching 25 to 30 hours a week, with the concomitant preparation that a teaching schedule demands? How do school management personnel find the time to assist in this process if they are locked into the customary kinds of disciplinary responsibilities, public relations activities, and the like?

As a consequence of such concerns the MSP Model recommended a flexible daily schedule for students based upon the previously discussed triangle of large groups, small groups, and independent or directed study. To assess whether changes in behavior were occurring and progress was being made toward the Model, a logging technique was developed to measure student activities. The following discusses the study's findings.

Student Activities

During the spring of 1974, a careful compilation was made of student activities through the use of a student log form. (Appendix C.) For one week the students compiled, with the assistance of their teacher-advisers, the activities which they undertook each school day. Twenty-three of the 29 Model schools, with a total pupil enrollment of more than 20,000 students, carried out this evaluation facet. What follows are some of the survey's pertinent findings.

The most common use of time, as shown in Table 1, was informal chatting and rapping (15.5 percent). Working

(10.8 percent) constituted the second most popular use of time, followed by listening to a teacher (9.9 percent). Obviously, students in conventional schools would report much more "real" time listening to teachers than one finds in the MSP schools. The percentages listed in other categories are an improvement over what one typically finds although further variation than indicated might have been desirable.

TABLE 1

Student Activities During the School Day
for One Week in the Time Study,
Spring 1974

Activity	Percent
Talking informally/rapping	15.5
Working	10.8
Listening to teacher	9.9
Listening to/watching other/viewing	8.9
Using equipment	7.7
Writing	6.8
Reading	6.7
Answering questions in writing/work sheets	5.1
Taking tests	5.0
Moving from place to place	5.0
Participating in discussion	3.5
Rehearsing/performing	3.4
Making something	2.9
Waiting	2.6
Thinking	2.4
Memorizing	1.7
Teaching others	.9
Scheduling or planning time	.7
Leading or making a presentation	.6

The preceding study of student activities was repeated in May 1975, with 14 schools participating in the study as contrasted with 23 schools in 1974. In 1975 the compilation of activities was changed slightly from the 1974 study. Whereas in 1974 a careful record had been kept in student log form, in 1975 a random sample of the use of student time and activities was conducted. At selected times during the day a student checked the activity in which he/she was

76

TABLE 2

M.S.P. TIME—ACTIVITIES STUDY

STUDENT DATA

School #		23 Sch	23 Sch	14 Sch	14 Sch	14 Sch	14 Sch
		1974 Mean	1974 Rank	1974 Mean	1974 Rank	1975 Mean	1975 Rank
ACTIVITY		Percent of time per week					
Listening to teacher	(1)	9.82	3	8.82	3	12.49	2
List./Watch./View.	(2)	8.87	4	8.13	4	8.94	4
Participating discus.	(3)	3.48	11	3.23	12	4.02	10
Making a presentation	(4)	.55	19	.50	19	.61	19
Reading	(5)	6.98	7	7.73	5	9.48	3
Memorizing	(6)	1.77	16	2.05	16	2.09	16
Taking Test		4.89	10	4.79	9	5.86	8
Writing	(8)	7.34	5	7.61	6	6.97	6
Answers/ Doing wk. sheets	(9)	5.12	8	5.50	8	7.91	5
Using equipment	(10)	7.23	6	6.78	7	6.39	7
Talking informally	(11)	15.02	1	15.72	1	13.28	1
General work/ service	(12)	10.84	2	11.32	2	3.18	13
Thinking	(13)	2.45	15	2.57	15	2.86	14
Rehearsing/ performing	(14)	3.31	12	3.51	11	2.80	15
Scheduling/ planning time	(15)	.74	18	.63	18	.77	17
Waiting	(16)	2.70	14	2.69	14	3.62	11
Moving— place to place	(17)	5.01	9	4.59	10	4.46	9
Making something	(18)	2.99	13	2.93	13	3.39	12
Teaching others	(19)	.85	17	.88	17	.73	18

presently involved. Table 2 contrasts both the mean and ranking data of the same 14 schools for the 1974 and 1975 studies.

As can be noted, "listening to teacher" ranked third in 1974 and second in 1975. "Listening to-watching others-viewing" ranked fourth both years of the study. There was a slight but not significant change in the amount of time devoted to "participation in discussion." The amount of time spent in "reading" ranked fifth in 1974 and third in 1975. Activities such as "memorizing" and "taking tests" remained approximately the same both years of the study. "Writing answers" and "doing worksheets" increased from eighth in 1974 to fifth in 1975. In both 1974 and 1975 "talking informally—rapping" ranked first throughout the project. "General work or service," which constituted 10.8 percent of the time in 1974 and ranked second, dropped to 3.18 percent and thirteenth in 1975.

Thus, the overall percentages which students spent in varied activities in 1974 and 1975 did not change significantly except for a slight reordering of the use of student time in the areas of reading, writing answers—doing worksheets, in general work or service, in rehearsing—performing, and in the amount of time spent waiting.

Pupil Options

As a result of the information derived through the diagnostic process, many MSP schools created a wide range of pupil options in each of the various areas of learning. Eventually, these options ranged from an increased number of elective courses to off-campus opportunities and mini-term arrangements.

For instance, during the third year of the Project, the registration handbook in one MSP high school included 160 different courses. This was a dramatic change from courses which existed when the Project was initiated. Approximately 70 percent of these courses were either a continuation (reinforcement) or an enrichment (in-depth) version of the courses taught during the first two terms.

The remaining 30 percent represented leisure-time activity education, such as backpacking, better boating, and folk dancing. Included were subjects that permitted students to explore possible interests.

Examples of the wide range of course options which became available to students during the third and fourth years of the MSP at one school were as follows:

Practical Vocational Division
- Child Development
- Buyers Beware
- Graphics
- Typing
- Photography
- Mechanical Drawing
- Electronics

Humanities Division
- A Knight's Hood Days
- English Literature, Old and New
- Lord of the Rings
- Asian-American Literature
- Of Human Interest
- Read and Tell
- Self and Others
- I'm OK, You're OK—Personal Growth
- If You Have the Will, We Have the Skill
- Thru the Poet's Eyes
- Beautiful Words
- Anthropology
- Peer Tutoring
- Wet, Windy, and Whipped

Math-Science Division
- Horticulture
- Marine Science
- Veterinary Science
- Forestry

In one school survey, 92.8 percent of the students indicated that with the Model they had the same or greater opportunity to study topics in which they were personally interested. In the same school all teachers agreed that such opportunities existed for students and that these options had not existed under the conventional program in which credit was based upon time rather than performance.

Departmental Activities During the School Day

In a further attempt to facilitate the development of the DPIE cycle, departmental activities during the school day were analyzed at various Model Schools. Careful review was made of the ways in which more time could become available for teachers to develop diagnostic and prescriptive materials.

The departmental activities reports assisted the teachers and their school-management teams in the analysis of new teacher roles. The reporting of the percentage of time allocated by each department to the various activities made it possible for the different curriculum areas of a school to discuss their allocation of time and to compare their utilization of time with similar curriculum areas in the other MSP schools (Appendix D).

During the third year of the Project a careful analysis was made of department activities. Following are some general findings based on reports from one school of how teachers spent their time during the week of the survey:

Curriculum Area	Findings
English	38% of time allocated to conferring about program, discussing in scheduled groups, informing and supervising.
Fine Arts	40% of time allocated to drilling/ coaching, informing, and supervising.

80

Mathematics	39%	of time allocated to supervising and informing.
Other Cultures	35%	of time allocated to discussing in scheduled groups, informing, and supervising.
Physical Education	43%	of time allocated to drilling/coaching, informing, and supervising.
Practical Arts	32%	of time allocated to informing and supervising.
Science	32%	of time allocated to informing and supervising.
Social Studies	37%	of time allocated to discussing in scheduled groups, informing, and supervising.
Religion	34%	of time allocated to advising/counseling, discussing in scheduled groups, and supervising.
All	19%	of time allocated to informing and supervising.

Teacher Activities During the School Day

During the spring, 1974, all teachers in 23 of the MSP schools kept a log of how they spent their time on the job during a one-week period. How teachers used time became significantly intertwined with the degree to which learning became more individualized. The results showed that the teachers spent approximately one-fourth of their school day in advising and counseling with students about individualized programs, in planning and developing individualized curricular schedules with students, and in related activities.

Individualized pupil scheduling without the constraints of conventional time arrangements in secondary schools was widely reported among the MSP schools. Scheduling

81

formats varied from time arrangements where pupil schedules were prepared individually for each day (depending on
the student's position on a growth profile) to semi-block
arrangements where changes were made periodically, such
as once or twice a week or every two weeks. In the Model
Schools Project individualized scheduling, which to a considerable extent indicated the degree to which learning had
become more individualized, was closely accompanied by
the successful implementation of the teacher-adviser role.

In several surveys conducted by independent auditors
at MSP schools, students were 100 percent in support of
the teacher-adviser role. Eighty-one percent of the students
favored the individualized schedules which were developed
through the teacher-adviser relationship. This resulted in
a substantial shift in the use of teacher time from the conventional format of lecturing or talking at students to a format of conferring with students.

Consequently, there was a significant change in the ways
in which teachers functioned. This shift was most pronounced in schools which implemented many facets of the
Model.

Degree to Which Teachers
Functioned Differently

For teaching to become a genuine profession, it is essential that teachers function differently. The concept of the
teacher as a source of wisdom resulting in the cycle of
"memorization, regurgitation, and forgetting" is inappro-
priate for a world in which learning must be a continuous,
lifelong process; a world in which some of yesterday's most
intelligent answers are not appropriate for today; a world in
which man must forever be pursuing new kinds of learning,
new kinds of information and knowledge in developing new
styles of life.

Teacher activities during the school day were systematically and thoroughly evaluated during the last semester of
the fifth year of the Project. The teacher log form was completed each day of the week and consisted of the type of
activity, with whom the activity occurred, how many persons were with the teachers, where the activity occurred,
and so on (Appendix E).

The listing below shows how all teachers in 23 MSP
schools divided their time among 18 activities during one
week. The most common activity, the one in which teachers spent 14 percent of their time during the week, was in
supervising (overseeing) students. The second activity,
with the same percentage, was informing (subject matter).
The remaining activities listed are shown in the order of
frequency. (The total was 96 percent, the 4 percent difference from 100 percent occurring during the process of
rounding numbers.)

Activity	Percent	Rank
Supervising (overseeing)	14	1.5
Informing (subject matter)	14	1.5
Relaxing and eating	8	3
Presenting (motivating)	7	4.5
Discussing in scheduled group	7	4.5
Planning and developing	6	6.5
Drilling and coaching	6	6.5
Doing clerical work	5	9.5
Conferring about program	5	9.5
Advising and Counseling	5	9.5
Evaluating people	5	19.5
Checking materials	3	13
Listening/observing	3	13

Conversing informally	3	13
Conferring about people	2	15
Developing professionally	1	17
Attending school activity	1	17
Evaluating program	1	17

This chart would appear to indicate that teachers' behaviors began to change through involvement in the Model Schools Project. Not all the evidence is encouraging, however. The fact that teachers spent 14 percent of their time supervising and another 14 percent informing (or presumably lecturing) was discouraging in the light of the goals of the Model Schools Project. The shift toward activities on the part of the teachers which enabled them to function as professionals and which humanized school climate was encouraging. It should be noted, however, that no indication is given of the quality of the activities, obviously a shortcoming in this type of evaluative approach.

In 1975 a similar study of the use of teacher time was conducted. Fourteen schools responded in 1975 as contrasted with 23 schools responding in 1974. The results of the 1975 study were as follows:

Activity	Percent	Rank
Informing (subject matter)	17	1
Supervising (overseeing)	10	2
Drilling and coaching	8	3
Discussing in scheduled group	7	4
Planning and developing	6	5
Advising and counseling	7	6
Presenting (motivation)	6	7
Relaxing and eating	6	8
Conferring about program	5	10
Evaluating people	5	10

Doing clerical work	4	11
Checking materials	3	12
Conversing informally	3	13
Listening/observing	3	14
Conferring about people	2	15
Developing professionally	1	16
Attending school activity	1	16
Evaluating program	1	18

It is apparent from the preceding data that some shifts occurred from 1974 to 1975. For example, "advising and counseling students" became a more significant priority among teachers. At the same time "drilling and coaching" increased significantly. There was a considerable reduction in the amount of time spent "relaxing and eating." Perhaps the work load of the program intensified in the second year. In other categories the reordering of priorities and the different use of time as indicated by the activities did not differ significantly from 1974 to 1975. Once again, no indication is given of the quality of the activities which leaves much to be desired in assessing the impact of ways in which time was utilized by teachers.

Teacher-Adviser Role

The teacher-adviser role, indicated through a variety of activities on the teacher log form, was one of the most important facets of the Model Schools Project, The close daily advisory relationship between a teacher and 30 to 35 students assisted the teacher in seeing the total educational program rather than merely seeing his/her own discipline, such as science, language arts, or music. The teachers became more understanding of the many forces which affected their students. Teachers saw pupils in the gestalt of learning rather than in the isolated learning of a given classroom or resource center. This kind of input was especially valuable for aiding teachers in the diagnosis of pupil needs.

In most of the MSP schools the entire student body was randomly and equally divided among the faculty for advising purposes. In some, members of the supervisory-management team also assumed their share of student advisees. The professional counselors conducted inservice training for teacher-advisers and handled specialized counseling problems. Either the teacher-adviser or the student advisee, however, could request a change if deemed appropriate. In other schools, each June the students could request any specific teacher as their adviser for the subsequent school year. Students who from past attitudes, behaviors, or problems proved that they needed special counseling were assigned to more experienced teacher-advisers or to professional counselors.

In one school, 87.6 percent of the students indicated they had the opportunity of choosing their own teacher-adviser. Students (81.2 percent) stated that teacher-advisers successfully helped arrange a schedule that suited their personal goals and educational needs.

The Model suggested that approximately five hours a week be available for each teacher to function as a teacher-adviser. The majority of schools struggled to provide this amount of time. Schools in which individualized scheduling became most pronounced did provide approximately five hours a week for the teacher-adviser function. In a survey at the close of the Project, 80 percent of the schools had implemented the teacher-adviser role to at least some extent. In most schools, from 90 to 100 percent of the students expressed positive reaction in their attitudes about the teacher-adviser relationship.

Research studies, such as that of Udinsky-Keefe-Housden, indicated there was a direct correspondence between the level of implementation of characteristics of the Model Schools Project and the extent of teacher-role change in those schools. As more and more characteristics of the

Model were implemented, teachers seemed to gather a broader base of understanding which assisted them in functioning not only as teacher-advisers but also in more effective ways as diagnostic-prescriptive advisers to individual students.

Activities of the
Supervisory-Management Team

A key factor in determining the excellence of any school program is the quality of those who provide leadership at the local school level. The concept of the administrative staff as a school-management team was a basic factor in the implementation of the MSP program. The principal was not seen in isolation from the supporting staff. The goal of 75 percent of the principal's time to be spent in instructional leadership was at the core of the Model's implementation. With such a time commitment, the principal could assist the staff in thinking through problems of diagnosis, prescription, implementation, and evaluation.

There was considerable evidence that MSP principals reorganized their school-management teams. Surveys done during the first two years of the Project indicated that principals quickly reorganized to make themselves available for curriculum leadership. This goal called for a substantial restructuring of administrative responsibilities, turning management-type activities over to other personnel.

Discussing how much time a principal spends as an instructional leader refers primarily to the use of time, not the quality of the use of that time. One project difficulty was that some principals who divested themselves of management activities had difficulty functioning as curriculum leaders. In an attempt to measure the quality of such a change, the S-M Team log form (Appendix F) was filled out by 23 school-management teams during a one-week period in the spring 1974.

The log report was limited to the activities of the S-M team during the school day in the week of the study. The data below present the order in which the activities appeared in the "S-M Team Log Form" with the percentage of time allocated to the activity by all the members of the S-M teams in the study. For example, since the item "developing professionally" appeared as activity one on the log, it is presented first. The average percentage of time spent in this activity by all the members of the S-M teams within the limits of the report was 2.18 percent. Once again, the limits of the report are the activities during that school day and in the one week of the study.

	Activity	*Percent*
1.	Developing professionally	2.18
2.	*Planning*	10.61
3.	*Supervising*	9.12
4.	Evaluating program	2.01
5.	Evaluating staff	1.60
6.	Evaluating students	2.92
7.	Recording and reporting	3.60
8.	Negotiating	.90
9.	*Counseling*	12.58
10.	Doing clerical work	6.36
11.	Checking on building and materials	2.62
12.	Disciplining	3.05
13.	*Teaching*	15.31
14.	Communicating	6.37
15.	Discussing	4.75
16.	Making a speech	.42
17.	Attending	1.26
18.	Relaxing/eating	6.92
19.	Attending meetings	5.41
20.	Traveling from place to place	1.99

In 1975, in a similar study, 14 rather than 23 schools supplied data on the use of time by the school-management

TABLE 3

M.S.P. TIME—ACTIVITIES STUDY
May, 1975

S-M TEAM DATA

School #		1974 23 Sch Mean	1974 23 Sch Rank	1974 14 Sch Mean	1974 14 Sch Rank	1975 14 Sch Mean	1975 14 Sch Rank
ACTIVITY		Percent of time per week:					
Developing professionally	(1)	4.95	9	5.04	9	1.22	18
Planning	(2)	12.17	1	11.74	2	16.77	1
Supervising	(3)	8.25	5	7.38	5	8.50	4
Evaluating program	(4)	1.93	16	2.00	16	3.97	11
Evaluating staff	(5)	1.24	17	1.31	17	1.96	15
Evaluating students	(6)	2.40	15	2.55	14	5.28	6
Recording & reporting	(7)	3.64	11	3.48	11	4.27	10
Negotiating	(8)	.96	18	.80	18	1.62	16
Counseling	(9)	10.66	3	9.58	4	11.43	3
Doing clerical work	(10)	6.91	6	6.77	6	5.22	8
Checking on building	(11)	2.89	13	2.71	13	2.23	14
Disciplining	(12)	2.52	14	2.11	15	1.54	17
Teaching	(13)	9.99	4	11.15	3	14.43	2
Communicating	(14)	6.03	8	6.21	8	5.65	5
Discussing	(15)	4.77	10	4.73	10	5.24	7
Making a speech	(16)	.63	19	.73	19	.33	19
Attending events/ meeting	(17)	10.83	2	12.07	1	3.12	12
Relaxing/eating	(18)	6.18	7	6.28	7	4.81	9
Traveling place to place	(19)	3.04	12	3.37	12	2.43	13

team. It should be noted that the 1974 study contained 20 categories, one more than the 1975 study. The data for "attending event and meetings" were consolidated so as to compare the total 1974 data with those of the 1975 study. The data in Table 3 include the mean and ranking for the total project of 23 schools who participated in the 1974 study; and the 14 schools who were involved in the 1975 study with both the mean and ranking data of these schools for the 1974 and 1975 studies.

As can be seen in Table 3, "planning" still occupied the majority of time in both 1974 and 1975. "Developing professionally" took a significant drop from ranking ninth among priority items in 1974 to ranking eighteenth in 1975. As might be expected, as programs developed, more time was spent in 1975 in "evaluating programs" than in 1974. In 1975 the school-management team ranked this activity as eleventh in importance contrasted with sixteenth. "Evaluating pupils" also became of much greater importance as programs were implemented. This ranked sixth in priority in 1975 and fifteenth in 1974.

The only other area of significant shift between these two studies was in "attending events—meeting," which shifted from second in importance in 1974 to twelveth in importance in 1975. Perhaps this is a reflection of better understanding of the program by the community, by teachers, and by students. Consequently less time was needed for public relations activities and attempts to explain and communicate the nature of the program.

The preceding information gives some indication of the prioritizing of time available to the school-management team. Studies like Udinsky-Keefe-Housden's show the school administration to be the most effective agency for implementing innovation in an environment of total change. The MSP teachers viewed administrative leadership as an important factor contributing to change.

The preceding study also stated that principals who wish to establish a total change environment within their schools

90

need to organize carefully to ensure optimum communication of administrative plans and adequate time to implement.

Numerous schools reported on the elaborate plans principals and the school-management team had made to meet with teachers to discuss all phases of the MSP design and to provide adequate clarification to all who would be affected by ongoing changes. The UKH study cited much ambiguity and lack of understanding among teachers and the school-management team. Building on these factors, the MSP developed a more extensive system of articulation and evaluation between a staff and its school-management team as the five-year Project unfolded.

Emerging Directions

Use of time by students, teachers, and the school-management team shifted substantially during the five-year interval of the Model Schools Project. Realistically, the DPIE cycle would not have become a reality without such a shift. The MSP schools made some sound initial steps toward developing a workable program of diagnosis, prescription, implementation, and evaluation of student growth both cognitively and affectively. Another system of evaluation utilized by many of the schools in the Project consisted of trained observers and school visits. These are discussed in the next chapter.

Suggested Activities

1. Visit a secondary school which has seriously sought to individualize instruction and briefly survey how students, teachers, and/or the school-management team spend their time. Which activities on the log forms found in this chapter receive the most time commitments? Which ones receive the smallest time commitments? How do your findings compare with the results reported in this chapter?

2. Based on your findings of the ways in which persons spend time in an innovative secondary school, what conclusions are you able to infer about the degree of individualization of instruction and personalization of human relationships found within that school?

8

Trained Observers and School Visits

The Model Schools Project employed numerous external auditors to assess and to provide feedback to the various schools as they gradually implemented newer ways of working with youth. What were some of the techniques and observations external auditors employed during their visits to schools, and what were their findings?

FOR MANY YEARS HIGH schools have been visited by a variety of persons external to the school itself. Often, parents have returned to school, especially during a public school week or a back-to-school night. In addition, regional accrediting teams and occasionally state department of education teams have visited selected schools. The accrediting process itself calls for an extensive visit by a representative group of external persons.

Historically, schools have also utilized outside consultant help from such sources as universities, the corporate structure, and governmental agencies. Sometimes a forward-looking principal has asked several other principals to spend some time in his or her school to assess informally the effectiveness of the educational processes taking place.

The exchange among principals working toward similar goals is invaluable. It is less threatening than visits by external visitors. It also enables principals to assist each other in staff inservice education. This type of self-help and cross-principalship tutoring helps both administrators and teachers grow.

The External Auditing Team

Early in the Model Schools Project, university professors and graduate students knowledgeable in educational innovations met for a two-day preservice session to discuss those parts of the Model which they as observers would assess during their visits to the various schools. (A listing of the areas and practices observed appears in Appendix G.) This initial external auditing process focused on program, people, and structure. The results were discussed with each faculty and were not released as general information for public consumption.

The observers found that some departments in the various secondary schools were making more progress toward implementation of the Project Model than others. For example, more progress had been made at the end of the first year in mathematics than in the fine arts. At the same time, administrators had dramatically altered their behaviors to fit the prescription of the Model. Clear progress had been made toward a school-management team concept with the principal spending 75 percent of his or her time in an instructional leadership role. Additionally, 11 of the 32 schools participating during the first year of the Project had adopted the teacher-adviser role. Little had been done, however, with individualized scheduling. Resource centers were beginning to emerge.

The MSP Project staff believed that an external auditing process could be useful if it kept a low profile and if its findings were treated with confidentiality. On the other hand, if the external auditing process was seen by school personnel as an attempt to be negative, the process was likely to be counterproductive. Consequently, extreme caution was taken in discussing and using the data gathered through the external auditing process.

An important function of any external auditing approach is to shift the emphasis (over a period of years) to a heavier focus upon internal kinds of evaluation. Thus, there is a shift from external to internal evaluation. Such was the case in the Model Schools Project.

At the close of the fourth Project year, the schools were asked to assess their own growth. The evaluation at this point highlighted (a) student and teacher contact through the teacher-adviser role and during independent study modules plus (b) student involvement in the learning process through physical participation, special interest options, and community learning centers. The results of the fourth-year internal analyses are found in Appendix H.

External auditors in the Model Schools Project received an array of different kinds of input. Interviewed were administrators, teachers in each of the eight or nine learning areas, the non-professional support staff, counselors, librarians, and students. Subsequently, each auditor wrote a summary of the school's progress in implementing the various aspects of the Model.

One concern which became obvious in the external auditing process was the role and preparation of the principal in providing the necessary kinds of leadership for a newer approach to education. One principal, for example, stated that he was concerned that the Model asked the staff to work at something that was impossible.

Another principal said, "I have a good grasp of the concepts involved in the Model because I have been reading the material for years, but I am not sure the faculty has the same conception as I have."

Still another principal said, "The staff knows what the Model is all about and while there are still some aspects that have not been fully worked out, the staff will be able to handle the situations as they arise. The greatest aspect of the program is the cooperation of the teachers—they work well together as departments and across departments."

Some of the summary comments were negative. Here are examples prepared by external auditors:

> Pockets of the staff have a good conception of the Model. Some of them worry about overcoming operational details. Some give the impression that they will go along with MSP, but they are not convinced it is what they should be doing. The administration is willing to let the staff solve their own problems and work on these solutions in isolation. There is not much interdepartmental coordination in overall curriculum planning. The staff seems enthusiastic, in fact, more so than the administration. There appears to be rigidity in following the Model, mainly because the Model says so, as if somehow it will work by itself . . . .

> The teachers, or at least the teams, seem to be left to their own devices as to how to implement the MSP . . . .

> The curriculum materials they have developed are more in the nature of assignment sheets. They are based on a single resource, usually the textbook, and do not have the ingredients normally found in more carefully designed packages.

In another school, the visiting team reported the following:

> There seems to be a high level of understanding for the MSP throughout the administrative hierarchy, decreasing in comprehensiveness as you go down the levels . . . .

> There is a distinct aura of optimism and there is nothing to indicate anything other than a positive feeling for the MSP and what the school was going to do or why it was going to do it. On the whole, the staff seems to be happy with the program, the changes it has brought. The staff is very friendly and is not

trying to hide feelings or shortcomings. They had pride with changes made and successes achieved in this program.

In a third report, the external auditors had this to say:

It was obvious that . . . this school and the entire staff are unique. All seem to be working cooperatively toward the same goal of doing everything they can to implement the MSP Model. This school has an attitude of willingness: willingness to work, to try something, to seek for solutions. The principal is extremely knowledgeable and his commitment to the Model and students is readily apparent. Although the entire staff may not have all the aspects of the Model firmly conceptualized, there appears to be enough of them to carry all the staff . . . .

One is left with the feeling that the Model will surely be fully implemented, that the administration and teachers will make it work. The students are full of expectations and in the meantime are learning a lot—not the least of which is that teachers are people—and having a good time in the process.

Another observation by an auditing team was as follows:

Having received some notoriety in the past for innovation, they seemed to feel that there was little reason to make major changes in what they are doing. Their primary concern at this point seemed to be aimed at how they might structure assignments for independent study. The small group meetings, on the whole, are just small, self-contained classes. There is an evident lack of team teaching and interdepartmental planning.

Such documented evidence collected in the various areas of Model implementation was invaluable. A key use of the information was to assist schools in developing plans for inservice programs for their school-management team, teachers, and pupils. Thus, the external auditing teams assisted in the process of formative evaluation so that plans could be made for more effective implementation of the Model.

In the second year of the Project, an incorporated group known as the Organization for Social and Technical Innovation (OSTI) was employed to function as external auditors to review the process and problems of implementing the Model Schools Project in six of the participating schools. These auditors spent two or more days talking with administrators, teachers, students, and aides about their early experiences with the Model Schools Project.

One of the primary goals of the OSTI auditors was to learn about the process and problems of implementing the Model in a variety of settings. Their purpose was not to assess the progress of any one school or to examine the educational effects of the Model, primarily because it was too early to say what those might be. Instead, they were looking at the process of adopting the Model in the six schools which they visited.

The report examined distinctions between schools, suggested some hypotheses about conditions which facilitated or impeded implementation, drew some general conclusions, and outlined alternative ways to act upon those conclusions.

The OSTI visiting teams tended to take a sociological and process orientation. They looked at the setting of each school in terms of social class, religion, race, economic level, and geography. They noted such variables as the size of the student body and the age of the school in attempting to determine the presence or absence of traditions and to learn more about faculty resistance to change.

The team also looked at the stages of implementation, noting the different ways in which schools first approached the Model. They examined external constraints or their absence, particular problems with the Model in different schools, and sampled the views of participants. The OSTI report was divided into two sections based upon the size of the six schools' enrollment plus their urban or suburban locale.

98

As a result of this auditing process, principals and faculties, individually and in groups, undertook extensive discussions about the progress they were making toward implementation of the Model. Efforts were made to understand the reasons for resistance toward the Model among teachers.

Some of the stated reasons were: moving from the security of a conventional classroom to independent study, fear of losing control of students, the demand for additional teacher planning time, lack of funds for the employment of aides, and occasionally faculties handicapped by their own cynicism and insecurity.

As a result of these findings, many schools attempted to enlist the talents of the strongest teachers on behalf of the Project rather than having them aligned against it. Plans were also made for greater involvement on the part of the students, including obtaining their views about the different ways in which they were learning and studying.

In attempting to cope with the need for more extensive curriculum materials, a finding of the OSTI study, the Project directors organized a clearing house which facilitated the distribution and sharing of such materials among the participating schools. Technical assistance also was provided to work with faculties in developing appropriate materials.

The OSTI report concluded:

The MSP appeared to have the potential for really turning on capable and dedicated teachers, those who were neither so inexperienced nor so embittered as to be immune to what the Model was offering. At last, teachers were given the chance to develop their own materials; watch and be watched by their colleagues in the business of teaching; feel released from the routine of five classes a day, five days a week; identify and develop their individual strength; and be finally adult in their professional lives.

99

In the last year of the Project, an intensive visit by more than 40 persons over a period of one month occurred at one of the MSP schools. These department of education representatives were sent to study this unique school and its efforts to individualize education. The dimensions of the study included an examination of the school's purposes and philosophy, its entire program as well as its supporting administration, its physical facilities, and its financial status. (See Appendix I.)

This external audit was made by a group whose majority were not oriented towards the kinds of individualized learning the Model Schools Project was committed to achieve. Comments made by the visiting state department team may also have been tempered by political considerations. Nonetheless, such input was of great value to the staff and school.

Other Types of External Evaluations

During the Model Schools Project, many of the participating schools established informal types of audits and visits, some of which resulted in written reports to the staff. Persons on external auditing teams came from neighboring school districts and universities, as well as from state departments of education. In most cases, the staff had follow-up discussions concerning the reactions of visitors.

Visiting auditors provided leadership for introducing various kinds of internal climate studies. As a result of information derived, the faculty in one school met every other week to discuss students who were having difficulties and to suggest ways in which they might be assisted. Consequently, the entire staff became involved in the process of shared decision making. Subsequent feedback from this faculty and others who had used similar techniques indicated considerable growth as a result of the actions which were agreed upon.

Other common kinds of evaluations by external visitors came from local university persons operating either as individuals or in teams. Such persons often had no previous knowledge of the Model and the process of individualizing education. Some visits were done in the early stages of the program and were mainly formative. These visits were to indicate the kinds of changes which should take place if the school were to achieve the Model. Towards the conclusion of the Project, efforts emphasized summative evaluation.

During one such evaluative visit a teacher said, "Paying paraprofessionals who are qualified teachers one-third salary is like running a sweatshop. You feel guilty and you depend on them and give them more responsibilities. I don't think it is proper, really, but it is what is best for the kids."

Another external auditor remarked that there was a sense of reluctance on the part of most teachers in one school to decrease the number of professionals in order to hire highly paid paraprofessionals. However, when the information was summarized, the external auditing team reported:

> Without considering the political and financial aspects of paraprofessional help, we asked: Does it work? The overall answer was "yes." The term most often used to describe such help was "invaluable." Teachers made such comments as, "We have all been helped immeasurably by student teachers. We would have dumped the program if they had taken them (the paraprofessionals and student teachers) away from us. The second year we had four aides and we did the most innovating."

In another school which was experiencing difficulty implementing the small-group discussion role, an external visitor was brought in to make recommendations for effective changes. His summary report indicated:

> There are both cognitive and affective outcomes of small group work which are not attainable in large group or individual work.

Increased personal responsibility for learning and receptiveness to the contributions of others can enhance these learning situations in important ways. Teacher-student and student-student interactions are also facilitated somewhat in a cooperative setting. For small groups to be most successful, however, there must be adequate planning, supervision, and participation. Teachers and students must be skilled in the techniques of small group work.

The preceding kinds of information were invaluable in helping teachers, school management personnel, and students to review a school's progress toward the Model. Obviously, inservice programs became more meaningful and more productive following such visits.

New Directions

In summary, the types of external audits discussed in this chapter were both a bane and a blessing. The motivation of visitors in a few cases appeared to be primarily political. Occasionally, the visits were cautious efforts by a variety of pressure groups in the community and by some teachers to discredit a relationship with the Model Schools Project and thus discourage its implementation. On the other hand, the vast majority of schools utilizing outside individual or team auditors did so to assist them in more effectively achieving the components of the Model and to improve conditions for learning.

The primary purpose of the use of trained observers and school visits by persons outside the Project as well as by the Project staff was to assist the cooperating schools in achieving their goal of becoming better schools. The evidence gathered during the Project indicated that the input by the university visiting teams, private corporate visiting teams, and directors of the Project proved to be highly valuable as a means of formative evaluation.

As a result of the information gathered through such visits, inservice education programs were developed, community orientation programs were organized and students were involved in more significant ways. Members of the school-management team reallocated their responsibilities and careful review was made of curriculum materials.

Perhaps the over-all impact of such visits was best summarized by one principal who said:

> As a result of the input received from both visitors outside of the project and those who were members of the project staff, our school is better able to respond effectively to the needs of our students. We have seen ourselves more accurately as others see us. Consequently, our educational product has been strengthened.

The next chapter is the first of three chapters, focusing on the interpretation of materials drawn from the six evaluative approaches discussed earlier. Chapter 3 discussed the stages schools went through in developing an understanding of and commitment to the Project, chapter 4 analyzed criterion-referenced data in relation to a school's program objectives, chapter 5 discussed progress toward the Model in MSP schools, chapter 6 reviewed the implementation of the Model via a diagnostic-prescriptive-implementation-evaluation cycle, chapter 7 presented additional research data as well as norm-based evaluation results, and chapter 8 discussed the observations of external, knowledgeable visitors.

Suggested Activities

1. Based on knowledge gained from a review of published survey forms and your own personal interests, awareness, and concerns, develop an observational instrument that could be used during a visit to a nearby secondary school. Prior to actually using your observational form or scale, ask for reactions and feedback from representatives of the school administration.

teaching staff, and student body. After making your observational visits, discuss your reactions and findings with an appropriate number of school representatives.

2. Discuss with a group of educators the strengths and weaknesses of using internal and external auditors to assess the growth and development of a school's educational program. Outline ways in which internal and external audit reports can be used beneficially to strengthen the educational program of a school.

9

Making Curriculum Decisions

Curriculum decision making is the heart of any school program. What are the priorities established in such decision making to determine the directions in which schools move? What priorities did the Model Schools Project establish in developing curriculum packages, in organizing for continuous progress learning, and in identifying essentials for all pupils? How did some schools involve their communities in curriculum decision making?

IF MEANINGFUL PROGRAMS relating to curriculum change are to occur, curriculum decisions must be made at multiple levels within a school system and involve large numbers of responsible people, including not only members of the school-management team, but also teachers, students, and community. For a number of years there has been talk about a teacher-proof curriculum. It is the author's opinion that no matter how well-prepared, well-written, or how thoroughly sequenced or packaged, a curriculum can never be considered apart from the persons who are its implementors.

Learning Packages

In the early stages of the Model Schools Project, schools faced the issue of prepackaged versus teacher-developed materials. Some schools compromised by utilizing pre-packaged materials which they felt were reasonably appropriate for their purposes and goals. This resulted in an individually-paced learning program but overlooked the element of personalizing or tailoring the curriculum to the disparate student population studying that field.

The danger in the use of curriculum packages is that they may result in a school being converted into a gigantic study hall, a school where absolute silence prevails as students thumb their way through one package after another. Such is not the intent of independent study as envisioned by the Model Schools Project.

In the initial years of the Project, quality control often was missing in the packages used. Too many, even today, offer an approach to learning with an exclusive focus on reading the printed page. Another serious limitation in the use of learning packages was the amount of teacher time required for their development.

One of the schools in the Project specified that learning packages or learning prescriptions should include the following characteristics:

- Performance objectives with specified performance levels based on departmental goals, usually stated in problem-solving terms so as to encourage a student's sense of discovery.

- A pretest (or an alternate form of the post-test) to permit students to "challenge" the unit, concept, or skill.

- The main idea or component ideas and sometimes a series of learning tasks breaking each complex concept or skill into a sequence of steps.

- Multiple resources and activities (print and non-print)

106

subject to student selection and sometimes including student-formulated alternatives.

- Various instructional modes to complement independent study (large group, small group, lab research, directed study).

- Provision for remedial activities and "quest" work at any stage of a sequence (quest being defined as self-chosen, in-depth study of a given concept, skill, or attitude).

- Self-tests to allow students to evaluate self-progress and goal achievement.

- Appropriate teacher evaluation of student achievement encompassing post-tests, oral evaluation, and student self-grading.

- An annotated bibliography, wherever appropriate, to serve as a guide for optional reading.

- A critique form to permit student evaluation of the effectiveness of the package or prescription.[1]

This basic checklist, developed by James Keefe, was also used to assess whether a learning prescription or package contained the *essential* structure for an adequate program of individualized instruction. However, it was not intended as an evaluation of the subject matter content of a unit. (See Appendix J.)

Efforts like these show that in spite of numerous problems, curriculum packages can offer multiple avenues to learning goals. Used in combination with a variety of other instructional media and methodologies, learning packages can facilitate both self-paced and personalized learning.

---

1. Chapter 4 discusses the means whereby the learning packages were evaluated and how the assessments led to better package construction.

Used in isolation from such consideration, however, they simply provide one more experience in educational boredom.

It is essential that school systems continue to develop disposable materials and learning packages, ones that can be prepared and modified with a minimum of input. This may mean moving from large packages in miniaturized textbook form toward the learning guide concept. No package, no curriculum sequence, and no learning guide can be adequate for any great length of time in a changing world.

Continuous Progress

Considerable sharing of ideas and materials took place among the Model Schools through extensive use of teleconference phones. In some cases, schools shared their learning packages so that it was not necessary for each school's faculty to reinvent the wheel.

One participating school system, because of the interrelatedness of the various levels of learning, was determined to sequence its curriculum from kindergarten through the twelfth grade, obviously a tremendous undertaking. This district began with language arts and mathematics and eventually sequenced objectives and goals for its entire population. While many of the materials were at level one of *Bloom's Taxonomy*, such an undertaking was nevertheless an impressive first step.

Although many schools implemented a continuous progress curriculum in one or more subject areas, very few programs were identical. One significant constant did exist, however—the removal of those chronological age barriers which lead to meaningless grade level groupings of youth, thus inhibiting genuinely individualized growth in learning.

In one four-year high school, the language arts curriculum was organized on a continuous progress basis. (See Appendix K.) A student's placement was determined through diagnosis followed by appropriate prescription. Once a student had attained minimal levels of competency in reading, spelling and vocabulary, oral communication, composition, and literature, he or she had options within or outside of the language arts department.

One teacher participating in this language arts program commented, "The continuous progress approach to the teaching of language arts holds tremendous promise for the individualization of instruction." Similar designs were used successfully in other schools.

Perhaps the effectiveness of any one program is best reflected in the ways students feel about it. The following paragraphs were written by a student after being involved in a Continuous Progress English program for one school year.

Some of the advantages of a non-graded English program, I think, are getting different teachers, and knowing just how different their personalities can be. To me, being with the same teacher for the whole school year or 180 days could be sort of boring. Last year where I lived, I had the same English teacher for the whole year and my teacher seemed very cold and didn't bother to meet any of us any further than to know our names. I also feel that having different teachers and different courses as one progresses through the curriculum takes the pressure off the student and makes the school year seem to go much faster.

It doesn't make the class seem too hard yet lasting too long. You have more and yet less time to concentrate just on one area. I feel comfortable in this system, due to the fact that the competition has vanished between the classmates and you have the chance of meeting your fellow upper-classmen if you are confident at that level. In some classes you might have a little fun, but in others it might be just one complete drag. I think it's a great opportunity to be in the same class with students at various grade levels

In their efforts to achieve a continuous progress curriculum, some schools initially used schedules with time constraints and moved gradually toward a total program of continuous progress education. Upon completion of the sequences and the achievement of the learning objectives, the student had the option of taking other electives or continuing an in-depth study in the common learnings area.

The experience of the Model Schools Project with continuous progress education indicates that such an approach promotes individualized instruction because it:

- Encourages students to master prerequisites.
- Eliminates needless repetition.
- Provides a tailor-made curriculum for each student.
- Acquaints the student with his particular strengths and weaknesses.
- Gives the student the opportunity to work with a variety of teachers plus the experience of working with students other than those at his/her own grade level.
- Gives the student a voice in helping determine his curricular experiences.
- Gives the teacher an opportunity to specialize in areas within his/her field of instruction.

Conventional schools can implement a partially individualized program on a transitional basis, as some of the Model Schools did, through slight modifications of certain departmental curricula. Transitional models or steps might include one or more of the following:

- Removal of grade designators.
- Removal of achievement grouping.
- Use of the DPIE cycle.
- Reorganization of selected components of a given curricular area.

Beyond considerations for such techniques as continuous progress education, curriculum sequencing, and learning packages, the Model schools were also basically concerned with questions of involvement. As one might expect, those schools which were most successful in implementing the Model were ones which had a very high level of involvement, including two-way communication with parents and the community at large.

In efforts to assess such feedback, Project schools used a variety of techniques. (See Appendix L.) In one school, strong parental support was given to the notion that children become more self-directed learners. A highly favorable parental attitude was also expressed toward the teacher-adviser or counselor role.

The learning package approach also had strong parental support; however, large-group presentations and small discussion groups were not viewed as favorably by parents responding to this questionnaire. They looked with favor on teacher conferences, including those with their child's teacher-adviser. As a result, the staff of this school held a series of meetings to design a better strategy for involving parents in curriculum decision making and for developing better lines of communication from the community to the school.

Curriculum development and curriculum decision making are highly complex and intricate tasks. They demand continuing input from all interested parties. If there is one basic lesson to be learned from the Model Schools Project, it is that all parties must be involved at all possible times.

This sounds like an impossible goal, yet it is a goal which was achieved to some extent by each of the more successful schools in the Project in their efforts to implement change. It is a goal which both conventional and innovative schools have found basic in relating to their various communities.

However, if the school is to achieve significant change, curriculum development and decision making must be accompanied by the different utilization of the "things" of education. This is the focus of chapter 10.

Suggested Activities

1. Organize a curriculum decision-making model for your school. Include the involvement of the school-management team, teachers, pupils, community persons, and parents.

2. Organize a plan enabling teachers in a particular department to develop a continuous progress curriculum. Include in such a plan the means of producing learning sequences, curriculum packages, and the other essentials in developing an individualized program.

10

Utilizing the "Things" of Education

Some educators see the process of change evolving in a piecemeal way. However, the MSP design called for a total commitment to change which would influence all educational components. With respect to structure, what did the Model Schools Project see as elements and what were their influence on a school's teaching-learning environment?

T HE SIX EVALUATIVE approaches utilized in this study to gather data provide information which gave increasing emphasis to the appropriate utilization of structural elements or the "things" of education. One of the basic tenets of the Model Schools Project was "doing better with what you have."

In other words, the Project directors believed that while schools could always use additional funding, the key to changing education is not to be found through large infusions of additional money. If education is to change significantly, it will change because students, teachers, community persons, and members of the school management team find

113

more effective ways to use present structures and the current "things" of education.

The Model Schools Project focused on program, people, and structure as the three key elements to a sound educational system. Structure as defined in this project consisted of:

- *Time*—individualized time for pupils, professionalized time for teachers;
- *Numbers*—size of learning groups, large groups, small groups, independent study;
- *Money*—ways in which funds could be allocated differently;
- *Spaces*—open, semi-open, or closed;
- *Things*—the options which exist in a school and its community to read, to view, or to listen.

Time.

The data gathered in this study indicated that unless time is used differently, individualization will forever remain a myth. Sitting passively, listening to teachers talk is not using time productively. On the other hand, having large numbers of students locked up in environments mistakenly called independent study (in reality, study halls) may also be a nonproductive use of time.

Previously cited evidence, for example, showed that principals quickly shifted their use of time in order to devote approximately 75 percent of their working day to curriculum leadership. Students also readily shifted their use of time from passive environments to active environments. By the third and fourth year of the Project, schedules were so reorganized that teachers had time to function as teacher-advisers and to work with individual students or clusters of students in helping to arrange personalized scheduling and individualized programs.

114

Some schools reduced the time teachers spent in lecturing, which is so characteristic of American secondary and higher education. Schools, furthermore, found a variety of ways to free teachers to work in preparing curriculum materials. Unfortunately, the typical structure of the American secondary school provides little time for these vital teacher and administrator activities. Three o'clock in the afternoon is hardly an appropriate time for meaningful kinds of staff development.

Numbers.

The ways in which schools view the size of learning groups is a critical variable in finding time for professional persons to break out of the conventional classroom syndrome. For many years there have been arguments pro and con about various sized learning groups. Considerable research has indicated that class size is not a significant variable in pupil learning. There are obviously educators who take an opposing point of view.

A basic belief of the Model Schools Project was that some materials can be communicated in large groups, others are most effectively communicated in discussion groups, and still other activities are best accomplished by one, two, or three individuals working in independent study environments.

The Project thesis was that a large group was any cluster of 15 or more students. Thirty was construed as being too small for most large-group instruction and too large for any small-group discussion. A key purpose of the Project was to eliminate the conventional class of 27 to 35 students.

Evidence accumulated during the Project indicated considerable variations among the schools in efforts to implement this concept. No conventional classes were found in those schools which were most effective in carrying out the Model. In the majority of schools in the MSP, however,

115

some conventional classes prevailed throughout the Project's five years. Without answering the questions of what are appropriate numbers of students to cluster for specific learning purposes, one cannot deal with the structural elements which seem to control schools and the use of time.

Large groups in the MSP typically ranged from 50 to 200 students. The size of such groups varied depending upon different educational goals, the age and readiness level of students involved, and certain cultural factors which influenced school environments. The primary purpose of the large group was motivational.

Small groups, focusing on discussion, ranged from six to 15 students. Here again, the exact size was determined by learning objectives and other local variables.

The percentage of time spent in independent study, the third element of the Model's team teaching design, differed among students. Some spent more than two-thirds of their time in a variety of learning resource centers at school and in the community. There were those, however, who spent little time in independent study because of a lack of basic skills and the inability to adjust to independent study environments. Several schools created "opportunity rooms" for such students while others generated rigid schedules to accommodate this small percentage of youth.

Money.

Information provided by numerous schools indicated that the majority spent no more money than their counterparts in the same school district. Nonetheless, participants did indicate that local "start-up" funds were essential for implementing something as different as the Model, including added funds for preservice and inservice activities, for building modifications, and for the purchase of new media-oriented materials.

116

Once each school had implemented the Model, however, its funding remained essentially the same as any comparably sized school in the district. The Model school participants allocated their monies differently, though, by spending funds on media rather than on books, by changing staffing ratios to make possible the employment of teacher aides, and by revising inservice education programs for all personnel.

Those schools that had received grants of $50,000 to $75,000 for involvement of staff progressed about the same as those that had received $10,000 or less. The key variable seemed to be the individual leader who directed the day-to-day operation of the MSP Program on the local level.

Spaces.

Many of the schools which were most effective in the implementation of the Model had older buildings with few provisions for large-group presentations, small-discussion groups, and independent study. While there were some schools in the Project which had new facilities, or at least new additions, most learned to use existing spaces in different ways. The buildings ranged from those designed specifically to accommodate the Model to facilities which were a compromise between conventional school buildings and those which would accommodate the Model's concepts.

One school, built in 1902, was remodeled during the five years of the Project. It is still an old building externally, but it is a radically different school internally.

The following guidelines for the use of facilities and spaces emerged from the Model Schools Project:

- Everything cannot be done at once.

- A good approach is to remodel three to six classrooms at a time as "open pods" permitting alternative approaches to education within the same building.

117

- Schools can use mini-modernizations as prototypes for more ambitious modernization projects.

- Often a change as simple as creating an arch between two typical classrooms will facilitate closer working together.

- District maintenance crews may do minor remodeling to get more return from normal maintenance budgets and eliminate the necessity for bond issues.

- More relaxed environments for learning may be created by use of bright colors, soft fabrics, carpeting, homelike lighting, etc.

- All who will use a remodeled facility should be involved in its redesign.

- It appears easier to change an old, outdated building to accommodate individualized instructional systems than to change new, already outdated facilities.

The Project was not entirely successful in encouraging personnel to abandon concepts that have dominated schoolhouse construction for generations. Nonetheless, there was more conscious effort to build facilities which would be a pleasant environment for learning. An example of this kind of effort was indicated by one school principal who said:

It seems appropriate to mention that change occurred in the minds of administrators, teachers, and students in a way that was as subtle as coloring a room. Two years ago the repainting of the school was started. The suggestion was made that as long as the school was opening minds to different methods of learning and a general openness of the minds of the whole school community, that the redecorating reflect the new school attitude. The new brighter colors certainly caught the attention of students, faculty, and visitors to the school. In every case, the walls of a room had at least two shades of a color if not two colors. The brightness seemed to have gone hand-in-hand with the excitement and enthusiasm of diversified learning opportunities.

Things.

The different use of the things in schools like educational supplies and equipment is essential if individualized instruction, within the reality of budget constraints, is to become a practice. Many of the schools in the Project did utilize money for different kinds of things than in the past.

There was extensive use in most of the Project schools of audio- and videotaping equipment where financially feasible. Most schools in the Project did not install expensive kinds of videotaping equipment and erasable tapes were purchased. As the Project progressed, more and more teachers prepared their own tapes, recording, among other things, their large-group presentations. In addition, tapes were prepared by students for use by their peers.

Disposable equipment systems, costing somewhat less money, are a guarantee against the obsolescence inherent in a fast-changing media field. Language labs are one example of an unwise expenditure of school equipment funds in the recent past.

Many Project schools made it possible for students to check out tapes as one would take a book from the library. The use of all kinds of media equipment increased dramatically, including slides, 16mm films, videotapes, and cassette tapes—a trend one sees in the larger American society as well.

Besides the typical work-experience programs, schools did not make much use of community space and things. With the exception of business education offerings and the new focus on career education, schools continued to duplicate equipment and materials which were more readily available in the community. Logistical problems such as transportation, supervision, and the inability to establish

119

appropriate relationships with community groups discouraged many school persons.

It is financially difficult, if not impossible, for a school to attempt to keep current with the "things" of education. These things may consist of business equipment, such as can be found in offices and computer centers, or they may consist of industrial equipment, such as can be found in laboratories and work-training areas. Tragically, many of the community vocational centers which were built during the past decade are instructing their students with equipment that is already obsolete.

It is unfortunate that in a time of financial austerity we have not yet learned to utilize the resources of our communities. Perhaps this is a reflection of the insecurity, the uncertainty, and the lack of know-how which exists within the profession. When schools develop this competency, they will significantly reduce certain kinds of facility costs.

The following represent some of the numerous building modifications that Project schools found can be made to accommodate sounder groupings of youth:

- Reduce overcrowding by introducing more large-group presentations, small-group discussions, and independent study areas:

  —Remove a wall between two classrooms and instead of school desks, arrange chairs in a semicircular fashion the length of the two rooms for large-group discussions; this facility houses twice as many pupils as in conventional classrooms.

  —Install two partitions in a conventional classroom to produce three small-group discussion rooms, substituting chairs in a circle for school desks; this arrangement accommodates 50 percent more pupils in the same space.

120

—Change classrooms into study and work centers for independent study; schedule more pupils for some supervised study and work in the community, with appropriate arrangements for accountability.

—Convert some wide corridor, lobby, and cafeteria spaces into independent study areas; pupils can walk through such areas while others are working, especially under flexible and individualized scheduled arrangements.

- Make better use of the potential talents of the professional staff:

—When a teacher retires or leaves, use the salary to employ clerks, instructional assistants, and general aides.

—Gradually increase the number of qualified adults who serve the pupils while reducing the number of certified teachers, simultaneously increasing the time that teachers have free from scheduled classes of pupils.

—Broaden the use of volunteer community aides and of cross-age tutoring.

- When funds are limited, use individual audiotape recorders and film projectors. Pupils benefit widely from personally and locally developed materials.

These suggestions can be used by both conventional and innovative schools in their attempts to alter structural elements. However, schools which provide additional spaces but no time to utilize these areas see few gains. Additionally, schools which provide many exciting "things" but do not come to grips with the questions of numbers and size of learning groups often have limited pay-off from their new gadgetry.

The results of the Model Schools Project indicate that flexing the use of time, money, numbers, spaces, and things in a coordinated, planned effort is far more likely to produce significant change than tinkering with these elements independent of each other. This is what the directors of the Model Schools Project called "putting it all together."

Suggested Activities

1. Design a theoretical secondary school facility for 200, 1,000, or some other number of students which incorporates the major concepts discussed in this chapter. Provisions should be made for instructional areas that house large groups, small groups, and independent study. Other considerations should include, but not restricted to, the following: administrative suites, counseling suites, teacher office areas, teacher and aide work areas, resource centers, etc.

2. Participate in the redesigning of an existing school facility or in the planning of a new school structure. Attempt to determine how the educational philosophy and desired instructional outcomes should influence the building plans. Visit other schools and note the ways in which programs have influenced facilities.

11

Putting It All Together

Reflecting upon the evaluative schematic of the Model Schools Project, what are its conclusions and what are its recommendations for improving schools in general?

THE PURPOSE OF THIS BOOK was to analyze the evaluative processes and findings of the five-year Model Schools Project. The heart of that Project was a new focus on individualized learning strategies via a reorganized school day encompassing large groups, small groups, and independent study in 32 junior and senior high schools in the U.S. and Canada.

The individualized learning base of the Model rested upon the interrelatedness of program, people, and structure. Thus the answer to the question, "How good is your school?" involves collecting and analyzing data relative to each of these three elements:

- The *program,* including curriculum content (both required and optional), the methods of teaching and learning, the locale where learning occurs, and the many facets of evaluation, both formative and summative.

- The *people* who aid the learners, including the instructional staff, the support services with a guidance focus, the school-management team, and the community.
- The *structure,* including the use of time, the organization of numbers, the ways in which money was spent, the school facilities, and the means whereby the system provided options or choices.

Earlier, the difference between conventional and mythological means of evaluation was discussed. Additionally, the purpose of evaluation, the necessity for staff understanding and commitment, and the appropriateness of various kinds of evaluative data, including criterion-referenced and norm-based data were analyzed. Furthermore:

- The fact that all schools follow a model, whether it be called traditional or innovative, was emphasized.
- The necessity for using a diagnostic-prescriptive-implementation-evaluation cycle, if schooling is to be individualized, was treated in some depth.
- The role of trained observers in aiding and assessing curricular change was presented.
- The processes for making curriculum decisions and the progress and problems encountered therein were highlighted.
- The ways in which the "things" of education could be utilized differently were delineated.
- The successes and failures of the participating schools in "doing better with what you have," the Project theme, were summarized.

Thus it was that the directors of the Model Schools Project, the principals, the teachers, the students, and communities involved in the Project sought to bring about genuine, realistic, badly needed change in structure, people, and program.

The concern nationally, on a grander scale, is that we in education will merely continue to change labels, that the banner on the marquee will be changed, but that nothing essentially different will happen behind the classroom door.

Through formative, evaluative processes, the Model was in constant metamorphosis. All were aware that many of the evaluative components needed to assess the kind of change effected in this project simply were not yet available. Schools were forced to improvise and utilize the best methods available at the time.

The nature of the teaching staff, the nature of the student body, the quality of a school's management team, the flexibility of the building, the support available at the central office level, the support of the community—these and many other variables make it unsound to compare School A with School B, even within a project such as this. The range of accomplishments in moving toward the goals of the MSP Model varied dramatically among the participant schools.

We must also move away from the concept that somewhere in America there are five, or 10, or 15 best schools. Best by what criteria? Using whose judgment and for whom?

The approaches used in gathering evaluative data in this Project are important because they focus on the real outcomes of the process called schooling, not superficial public relations outcomes, many of which were discussed in chapter 1. They are more effective ways to measure the unique contributions that a secondary school may have made to a student's growth.

The focus in the evaluative methods used in the Model Schools Project has been to assist the individual student in

125

his growth through an appropriate diagnostic and prescriptive cycle. The emphasis has been to aid schools in comparing themselves to where they were yesterday, to where they are today, and where they may be in the future.

Considerable emphasis has been given throughout this book on careful identification of the purposes of both schooling and evaluation. A well-defined philosophy, clear-cut goals and objectives, a specified curriculum model, a systematic evaluation design, both formative and summative, and communication channels through which the results are made clear to school staff and public have been stressed. The evaluative approaches in this study can be used by any school, conventional or otherwise. They will assist in providing better information to answer the question "How good is your school?"

Project Findings

The findings of the Model Schools Project, in many ways similar to those reported in other studies, may be summarized as follows:

1. The key person in the change process is the building principal.

2. While collective district efforts may assist and support, change still is basically a process to be undertaken by a local faculty, its school-management team, its pupils, and its supporting community.

3. Evaluation must focus on where the school is and where it is going. It must naturally indicate individual pupil growth as well as school growth. Little is to be gained, however, by comparing one school with another or one student with some abstract nationalized norm.

4. Evaluation must reflect a broader spectrum of the objectives of a school. Beyond simplistic measurements,

evaluation should reflect such significant variables as integrity, continuing desire to learn, and attitudes toward oneself and society.

5. The amount of money received by an individual school has little significant relationship to its success in implementing change.

6. The rate of change among MSP schools appears faster in schools in middle-sized suburbs.

7. Strong commitment from boards of education and district-level persons with some supporting resources becomes an increasingly essential ingredient for the success of an innovative project.

8. Changing the behaviors of school-management teams, teachers, and pupils is a complex task. It demands both emotional and cognitive input.

9. Implementing change successfully necessitates both commitment and understanding on the part of all persons. The level of involvement must be extensive and continuous.

These findings, especially as they relate to the change process, are discussed more completely in another MSP book, *How To Change Your School.*

The Future

It is difficult, in many respects, to know what the nature of schooling will be tomorrow, but there are some indications on the horizon which must be reviewed as we attempt to modify current school systems. Survival today is of little value if we live a schizophrenic, shattered tomorrow. As sound as the concepts of the Model Schools Project may have been, they may not be adequate in the future.

Many additional educational alternatives are emerging as school systems seek to better meet the needs of their clientele. For example, we may see an increasing movement toward "disposable school systems," a concept implying that no school, no model, no definition of prescribed and optional learning environments today can expect to endure. This is in marked contrast with many of the yesterdays where a kind of stability was sought and found in what was then known as current practice.

Beyond the clatter of "deschooling" we will undoubtedly see substantial changes in the organizations of systems for learning. We will see the increased adaptation of practices which base credit upon performance, not upon time. We will see increasing application of the process of diagnosis, prescription, implementation, and evaluation rather than having all persons start at the same point, exposing them to the same experiences, and expecting equal achievement at the same time. We will see increasing emphasis upon life-long learning for all people in our society.

We will see an increasing capacity for adaptation on the part of persons involved in the process called schooling. The kinds of unique adaptive capacities we have seen multiplying in the industrial and corporate structure might well become true in education.

We will undoubtedly see many starts and stops in the movement toward recognizing each person as an individual with individual needs, with individual paces of learning, with individual kinds of interest, and with individual momentum. We will not awaken, as a long dormant Rip Van Winkle, to a sudden sunrise when all education will be individualized.

Different and more sophisticated methods of evaluating individual progress of students, teachers, and supervisory-management team members will also produce improved methods of program evaluation.

The miracle of individualized instruction will not occur tomorrow, but through hard work and diligent application, it may emerge in the decades ahead. Then, and then only, it may be possible for us more accurately to answer the question, "How good is your school?"

Suggested Activities

1. Any comprehensive change in education necessitates "putting it all together." It also requires significant involvement of many concerned and responsible elements in the community. Based on your community and its needs, how would you go about identifying and involving such groups in order to ensure maximum understanding and support?

2. Now that you have read this book, take some time to organize and express in writing your personal reactions and thoughts. What contributions might you make in the evaluation of schools which seek to answer the question, "How good is your school?"

Appendix

A. STUDENT AND TEACHER ATTITUDES TOWARD THE MODEL SCHOOLS PROJECT

Student Attitude

This section of the study is concerned with attitudes. Below you will find twenty statements expressing different attitudes about the Project. Please mark your answer sheet as follows:

Mark "0" if you *agree* with the statement

Mark "1" if you *disagree* with the statement

Try to indicate either agreement or disagreement with *each* statement. If you cannot decide about a statement, you may indicate your uncertainty by marking "2" on the answer sheet.

(This section includes #44-63 on your answer sheet)

44. Large-Group Presentations are pleasure presentations.

45. I really don't like anything about the Model Schools Project.

46. More individual time with the teachers is a great help to learning.

47. Students are too much on their own.

48. Independent Study is the best way to learn.

49. Large-Group Presentations should be elective.

50. Independent Study is not much better than Study Hall.

51. Getting information from another student is no longer called cheating.

52. Attendance should not be required for Small-Group Discussions.

53. Under the Model Schools Project work is paced to the individual student.

54. It is hard for me to organize my study habits now that I am more on my own.

55. I can catch up if I've been lazy for a while.

56. All students should study the same thing at the same time.

57. Using learning packages helps the student learn responsibility.

58. It is easier to learn if you can take the test when you are ready.

133

59. Small-Group Discussions are a waste of time.

60. Learning improves when a student is told about his mistakes rather than getting a failing grade.

61. Independent Study doesn't give enough teacher help.

62. Some guys do all the talking in the Small-Group Discussions.

63. Individual time spent with instructors adds nothing to the learning situation.

Teacher Attitude

This section of the study is concerned with attitudes. Below you will find twenty statements expressing different attitudes about the Project. Please mark your answer sheet as follows:

Mark "0" if you *agree* with the statement

Mark "1" if you *disagree* with the statement

Try to indicate either agreement or disagreement with *each* statement. If you cannot decide about a statement, you may indicate your uncertainty by marking "2" on the answer sheet.

(This section includes #44-63 on your answer sheet)

44. Small-Group Discussions should be abandoned.

45. There is difficulty on the part of parents in accepting and interpreting new forms of reporting student progress.

46. The Model Schools Project concept of individualized scheduling is a new form of rigidity imposed upon the student.

47. In the Model Schools Project the slow child can experience a sense of accomplishment.

48. Students do not know enough about the subjects to discuss them intelligently in Small-Group Discussions.

49. Implementation of the Model Schools Project requires summer workshops for teachers.

50. The Model Schools Project favors the abandonment of traditional A,B,C,D,F grades in the evaluation of student progress.

51. Teachers do not possess the skills required for effective motivational Large-Group Presentations.

134

52. The Model Schools Project eliminates inter-student competition.

53. The increased number of adults in a school gives stability to the Model Schools Project.

54. A serious problem arises from a partial implementation of the Model Schools Project.

55. Under the Model Schools Project slow learners are less stimulated to complete their learning activities.

56. The Model Schools program helps to draw an entire staff together.

57. The Model Schools Project curriculum keeps students in constant contact with the basic areas of human learning.

58. Individualized scheduling makes it possible for teachers to have more time for planning.

59. Students consider Small-Group Discussions to be a waste of time.

60. The Model Schools Project demands more expenditure of teacher time than does the traditional school.

61. Teachers are disturbed by their inability to keep accurate record of students moving about.

62. Para-professional help does not foster better education.

63. Compulsory attendance at Large-Group Presentations destroys student enthusiasm and motivation.

SECTION III: FACTORS INFLUENCING CHANGE

The Model Schools Project (MSP) sees the teacher functioning in the role of "facilitator of learning"—a director of learning strategies. Below are listed (in alphabetical order) two sets of factors which teachers in MSP schools have identified as having *contributed* to or as having *interfered* with the implementation of this new teacher role.

On the following items, please mark 0-4 to indicate your choice.

(This section includes #64 and #65 on your answer sheet)

64. Indicate which *one* of the following factors you believe has *contributed* most to the implementation of this new teacher role.
    0 Administrative leadership and encouragement
    1 Differentiated staffing and team teaching
    2 Individualized instruction
    3 Time for student independent study
    4 No one factor

65. Indicate which *one* of the following factors you believe has *interfered* most with the implementation of this new teacher role.
    0 Inadequate facilities
    1 Insufficient aides
    2 Lack of time
    3 Shortage of funds
    4 No one factor

B. COGNITIVE AND AFFECTIVE
GROWTH OBJECTIVES

Objectives

Following is a review of the objectives as established for pupil and teacher evaluation.

1. *Cognitive Method:* Student
   By the end of the 1973-74 school year, a minimum of 80 percent of the groups in each level will attain not less than a mean average of 105 on processes characteristic of individualized instruction as indicated by the Process Index of Individualized Instruction. (Note: Level I is equivalent to Grade 10; Level II, Grade 11; and Level III, Grade 12).

2. *Affective:* Organization: Student
   By the end of the 1973-74 school year, a minimum of 80 percent of the groups in each level will attain not less than a mean average of 120 in the assessment of the organizational environment as indicated by the High School Organizational Environment Inventory.

3. *Cognitive:* Method/Facility: Student
   By the end of the 1973-74 school year, a minimum of 80 percent of the groups in each level will attain not less than a mean average of 52 on the utilization of human and learning resources as measured by the Study Habits and Skills Test.

4. *Cognitive:* Method: Student
   By the end of the 1973-74 school year, a minimum of 80 percent of the groups in each level will attain not less than a mean average of 100 on creative approaches as indicated by the Group Test of Creativity.

5. *Affective:* Organization: Student
   By the end of the 1973-74 school year, a minimum of 80 percent of the groups in each level will attain not less than a mean average of 410 on the development of positive attitudes as indicated by each subtest in the Meaning of Words Inventory.

6. *Cognitive:* Method: Teacher

   By the end of the 1973-74 school year, a minimum of 80 percent of the teachers will attain not less than a median of 105 on processes characteristics of individualized instruction as indicated by the Process Index of Individualized Instruction.

7. *Affective:* Organization: Teachers

   By the end of the 1973-74 school year, a minimum of 80 percent of the teachers will attain not less than a median of 120 on the assessment of the organizational environment as indicated by the High School Organizational Environment Inventory.

8. *Affective:* Organization: Teacher

   By the end of the 1973-74 school year the teachers will attain not less than a mean average of 4.0 on the development of positive attitudes toward change as indicated by each pair of bipolar adjectives in the subtests of the Meaning of Words Inventory.

C. STUDENT LOG FORM

What
Advisory Group/Homeroom/TA
Lunch/Relaxation/Clubs
Job/Community Experience
School Service
English
Mathematics
Social Studies
Science
Other Cultures (foreign language)
Practical Arts (bus., home ec.,
indus. arts)
Fine Arts (music, drama, art)
Health, Fitness, Recreation (PE,
athletics)
Religion (for nonpublic schools
only)
Discipline/Detention

Where
Home
School
Community

Activity
Listening to teacher
Listening to/watching
viewing
Participating in discussion
Leading or making a presentation
Reading
Memorizing
Taking tests
Writing
Writing answers/doing work sheets
Using equipment
Talking informally/rapping
General work or service
Thinking
Rehearsing/performing
Scheduling or planning time
Waiting
Moving from place to place
Making something
Teaching others

Why
Assigned by teacher
My own choice

Type
Subject related
Not subject related

How Many
1 (Just myself)
2-6
7-15
16-40
41 or more

Help
Teacher
Other adult
No adult

Value To Me
High
Medium
Low

What Happened
Learned something
Put to use something I learned
before
Made me think differently
Did or made something special
Helped someone or the school
Made something
Not sure

Feeling
Enjoyed doing something
Did not enjoy it

---

*Space is provided on the form for the
participant to indicate the time allotted
to the different items during the school
day and outside the school day.*

D. SUMMARY – DEPARTMENT ACTIVITIES

	1 ENGLISH		2 FINE ARTS		3 MATHEMATICS		4 OTHER CULTURES (FOREIGN LANG.)		5 PHYSICAL EDUCATION	
ACTIVITY	Rank Order	% of Time	Rank Order	% of Time	Rank Order	% of Time	Rank Order	% of Time	Rank Order	% of Time
1—Advising/counseling	9	5.7	9	4.7	11	3.6	10	4.2	9	4.5
2—Conferring about programs	3	8.9	10	4.7	6	5.8	14	2.4	13	4.5
3—Conferring about people	15	2.4	17	1.4	15	1.7	17	1.8	15	1.3
4—Discussing in scheduled group	2	9.6	8	5.0	7	5.3	3	10.0	14	4.9
5—Drilling/coaching	14	2.9	2	13.2	9	4.2	4	9.1	2	4.7
6—Informing (subject matter)	4	8.7	3	9.1	1	27.7	1	13.8	3	15.0
7—Presenting (motivation)	5	8.0	5	7.5	5	6.1	5	8.6	8	7.7
8—Supervising (overseeing)	1	10.6	1	17.4	2	11.4	2	11.6	1	17.9
9—Developing professionally	16	2.0	15	1.8	18	.8	15	1.9	16	1.6
10—Planning and developing	8	6.1	6	6.0	4	7.0	9	5.4	7	5.9
11—Evaluating programs	17	1.8	18	1.2	17	1.5	16	1.8	18	1.0
12—Evaluating people	10	5.7	11	3.9	10	4.2	7	6.3	5	5.3
13—Listening/observing	11	4.7	12	3.8	16	1.5	11	2.8	10	2.9
14—Conversing informally	13	4.0	14	2.4	14	2.0	12	2.8	11	2.0
15—Relaxing and eating	6	7.7	4	7.9	3	7.6	6	7.9	4	9.1
16—Checking materials	12	4.0	13	2.9	12	2.4	12	2.8	12	4.2
17—Doing clerical work	7	6.2	7	5.6	8	5.1	8	5.6	6	5.6
18—Attending school activities	18	1.2	16	1.5	13	2.2	18	1.3	17	1.5

ACTIVITY	6 PRACTICAL ARTS Rank Order	% of Time	7 SCIENCE Rank Order	% of Time	8 SOCIAL STUDIES Rank Order	% of Time	9 RELIGION Rank Order	% of Time
1 – Advising/counseling	11	4.5	9	4.4	9	4.8	2	11.8
2 – Conferring about programs	8	5.0	7	5.8	11	3.4	5	8.0
3 – Conferring about people	17	1.3	15	2.0	15	1.8	12	3.5
4 – Discussing in scheduled group	9	4.9	4	7.8	3	11.6	1	13.0
5 – Drilling/coaching	10	4.7	13	2.9	14	2.9	9	4.5
6 – Informing (subject matter)	2	15.0	2	15.3	2	11.9	6	6.9
7 – Presenting (motivation)	4	7.7	6	6.5	5	9.1	7	6.8
8 – Supervising (overseeing)	1	17.9	1	17.5	1	13.6	3	9.5
9 – Developing professionally	15	1.6	16	1.3	17	1.3	17	1.4
10 – Planning and developing	5	5.9	5	7.0	6	7.3	7	6.8
11 – Evaluating programs	18	1.0	17	1.3	16	1.5	18	.8
12 – Evaluating people	7	5.3	8	4.6	8		10	4.1
13 – Listening/observing	13	2.9	12	3.3	10	3.7	13	3.5
14 – Conversing informally	14	2.0	14	2.5	13	3.0	15	2.4
15 – Relaxing and eating	3	9.1	3	8.7	4	9.2	4	8.2
16 – Checking materials	12	4.2	10	4.2	12	3.4	16	1.9
17 – Doing clerical work	6	5.6	11	4.0	7	5.4	11	4.0
18 – Attending school activities	16	1.5	18	1.1	18	.9	14	3.0

E. TEACHER LOG FORM

Activity
Advising/counseling
Conferring about program (curriculum, etc.)
Conferring about people
Discussing in scheduled group
Drilling/coaching
Informing (subject matter)
Presenting (motivation)
Watching, controlling
Developing professionally
Planning and developing
Evaluating program
Evaluating people
Listening/observing
Conversing informally
Relaxing/eating
Checking materials
Doing clerical work
Attending school activity

With Whom
Self
Students
Teachers
Department members only
Guidance counselors
School administrators/supervisors
Non-certificated personnel
Parents
Visitors
Community resource people
Central office personnel
Student teacher

How Many Students With You
None
1
2-4
5-15
16-40
41+

Where
School
Home
District Office
Another School
Community

Value To Me
High
Moderate
Low
None

Outcome
Learning materials
Learning strategies (system, plan)
Presentations
Evaluation tools
Evaluation reports
Decision process assisted
Solution to problem
Anxiety reduction/catharsis
Concept, skill, attitude acquired
Budget, policy, document (letter, bulletin)
None
Other (specify on reverse side of sheet)

Perception of Effect on Others
Stimulating
Little effect
No effect

Space is provided on the form for the participant to indicate the time allotted to the different items during the school day and outside the school day.

F. S-M TEAM LOG FORM

Area of Concern
School/Plant Management
Budget
Instructional Personnel
Pupil Personnel
Community Relations
Student Activities
Curriculum and Instruction
Personal

Activity
Developing professionally
Planning
Supervising
Evaluating program
Evaluating staff
Evaluating students
Recording and reporting
Negotiating
Counseling
Doing clerical work
Checking on building and materials
Disciplining
Teaching
Communicating
Discussing
Making a speech
Attending events/meetings
Relaxing/eating
Traveling from place to place

With Whom
Self
Students
Teachers
Principal
Other supervisory management
     team
Non-certified personnel
Parents
Resource people outside school
Central office personnel
Salespersons
Other visitors

How Many With You
Alone
1
2-4
5-15
16 or more

Where
School
Home
Community
Out of town
Central office/Other schools

Value To Me
High
Moderate
Low

Outcome
Diagnosis
Plan/design
Solution to problem
Change effected
Evaluation
Concept, skill, attitude acquired
Input/feedback
Task completed/Other (specify on
     reverse side)
None

*Space is provided on the form for the
participant to indicate the time allotted
to the different items during the school
day and outside the school day.*

143

G. SUCCESSFUL APPROACHES AS REPORTED BY MSP VISITORS

SCHOOL NO.	English Language Arts	Drama	Fine Arts	Art	Music	Health, Fitness, Recreation	Mathematics	Other Cultures	Practical Arts - Vocational	Industrial Arts	Home Economics	Driver Education	Business Education	Religion	Social Studies	Science	Activity Programs	Large Group Instruction	Small Group Discussion	Independent Study	Pupil Progress Reporting	Administrators	Public Relations	Teacher-Advisor	Professional Counselors	Aides	Flexible Scheduling	School Facilities	Resource Centers	Media
1					X											X				X		X				X				
2					X											X														
3	X	X		X	X		X		X							X		X	X			X		X					X	
4																														
5	X																					X								
6								X																						
7						X																X								
8																		X				X		X						
9																		X				X		X						
10					X													X	X		X					X	X	X		
11					X					X		X								X		X								
12																														
13					X			X																				X		
14	X																													
15																			X			X		X					X	X
16			X						X		X	X										X		X						X
17					X			X		X		X			X	X					X	X	X	X					X	X
18	X						X							X			X		X	X	X	X		X			X	X		
19	X															X			X		X	X		X						
20																														
21			X																			X		X						
22	X												X																	X
23	X			X	X										X			X	X	X	X								X	
24					X		X															X	X	X	X				X	
25					X	X			X					X															X	
26					X				X	X					X														X	
27											X		X							X										
28																														
29																								X						
30																			X			X			X		X			
31																											X		X	
32	X					X																								

144

SCHOOL NO.	1. Instructional Leadership	2. Expenditures Compared to 1971-72	3. Students per Adult	4. Students per Teacher	5. % of Teacher-Advisers (100%)	6. Teacher Time Spent on Advisees (5 hr/wk)	7. Teacher Time with Students in Independent Study (6 hr/wk)	8. Professional Counselor Time Working with Teachers (5 hr/wk)	9. Reduction of Required Curriculum	10. Continuous Progress Arrangements	11. % Students Enrolled in Community Learning Centers	12. % Student Contact with All Curricular Areas (100%)	13. % Students Pursuing Special Interest Projects (100%)	14. % of Student Time Spent Physically Doing Things (25%)	15. % of Student Time Spent Listening to Teachers (5%)	16. % Students Receiving Only Letter Grades (0%)
1		S	26	32		+	+					+		+	+	
2		S	16	17	+		+	+						+		
3	-	-	-	-	-	-	-	-	-	-	-	-	-	-	-	-
4	+	m	11	32	+	+	+	+		+	+	+	+	+	+	+
5	+	m	12	175			+									
6		s	14.5	25.5	+	+	+	+	+	+	+		+	+	+	+
7	+	s	17.6	26.5	+				+	+	+	+	+	+		
8		L	16	18.2	+	+					+			+		
9	+	m	15	22	+	+	+					+		+		
10		s	12	22	+	+	+	+				+		+	+	⊤
11	+	m	16.5	32	+		+	+	+				+	+		
12		s	16.4	17.3	+		+							+		
13		s	19	25	+									+		
14	+	m	23	27			+					+		+		
15	+	s	20.5	26.5	+		+			+		+		+		
16		m	12	26	+	+	+		+	+		+		+	+	+
17		L	15	29	+	+	+	+	+	+	+	+	+	+	+	+
18	+	s	14.5	17.5	+					+		+		+	+	+
19		s	9.3	21.3	+	+	+			+	+	+		+	+	+
20		m	13	17										+		
21	+	s	20	24	+									+		
22		s	16	30	+					+				+		
23	+	s	12	23	+	+			+			+		+		
24	+	s	20	20	+		+	F	+	+				+		
25	+	s	19.4	23			+							+	+	
26		L		25			+							+		
27		s	17	23	+											
28	+	s	12	29	+	+	+	+		+				+		
29		s	10	21	+	+	+	F						+		
30		s	17	25	+						+			+		+
Ave		s+	15+	24+												

An analysis of the preceding fourth year internal report indicated:

1. *Instructional Leadership*
    Out of the 30 Supervisory Managerial tasks five were selected

145

as evidence of positive instructional leadership. (Items 1, 3, 21, 22, 24.) Fourteen items were designed as negative contributors to instructional leadership. (Items 7, 8, 9, 11, 13, 14, 15, 16, 17, 20, 25, 26, 27, 31.) One point was assigned to each positive task which was performed and to each negative task which was delegated to another administrator. A score of 16 out of 19 (approx. 85%) was given a + rating.

2. *Expenditures*
   S = Same as in 1971-72
   M = More than in 1971-72
   L = Less than in 1971-72

3. *Students per Adult*
   The number reported is the actual number of students for each adult. The Models calls for approximately 15.

4. *Students per Teacher*
   The number reported is the actual number of students for each teacher. The Model calls for 30-35.

5. *% of Teacher - Advisers*
   A + is recorded for schools that have 85% or more of their teachers serving as TAs. The Model goal is 100%

6. *Teacher Time Spent on Advisees*
   On the basis of a 30 hr. work week the Model recommends that teachers spend approximately 5 hours per week serving as an Adviser. A + was recorded for schools where teachers devote an average of 4-6 hours per week as a TA.

7. *Teacher Time With Students in Independent Study*
   The Model recommends that teachers spend 6 hours in a 30 hour week, working with students during their Independent Study Time in learning centers. A + was given for a school average of at least 5 hrs. per week.

8. *Professional Counselor Time Working With Teachers*
   As a result of the TA role professional counselors should be spending more time aiding teachers and less time performing conventional tasks such as scheduling, etc. A + was given for designating a total of 4.5 hours or more on items 4.24 and

146

4.25 combined. (The 4th Yr. Report average was 3.4 hrs. per week of professional counselor time aiding teachers.)

9. *Reduction of Required Curriculum*
   One point was recorded for each curriculum area that reported "considerable" progress in reducing content. One-half point was recorded for each curriculum area that reported "some" progress. A + was recorded for schools receiving a score of 85% or better on scale of 8/9.

10. *Continuous Progress Arrangements*
    The score was computed exactly as in item #9.

11. *% of Students Enrolled in Community Learning Centers*
    The 4th Year Report showed an average of 10% of all MSP students engaged in out-of-school learning centers. The percentage for individual schools ranged from 51% to 0% A + was recorded for schools having at least 10% of their student bodies participating in out-of-school learning centers.

12. *% of Student Contact with All Curricular Areas*
    The Model recommends that all students be involved in the 8-9 major curriculum areas in a continuous basis. A + was recorded for schools that provide at least 85% involvement in all curricular areas.

13. *% Students Pursuing Special Interest Projects*
    The Model recommends that *all* students should have time and be encouraged to pursue projects of special interest. A + was given schools that have 50% or more students pursuing special interest projects. (The average for the 4th Year Report was 32%.)

14. *% of Student Time Spent Physically Doing Things*
    The Model recommends that 25% of a student's learning time in independent study be comsumed in actually "doing" things—not passively listening or reading. A + was given to schools that met the goal of 25% (The average of the 4th Year Report was 27% on this item.)

147

15. *% of Student Time Spent Listening to Teachers*
    The Model recommends that 5% of a student's learning time
    be spent listening to teachers. A + was given to schools that
    had an average of 7% or less. (The average 4th Year Report
    on this item was 10%.)

16. *% of Students Receiving Only Letter Grades*
    The Model recommends that 0% of the students receive
    only letter grades. A + was recorded for schools that
    achieved the MSP goal of 0%.

I. VISITING TEAM COMMENDATIONS AND RECOMMENDATIONS

Commendations

1. The staff and pupils are to be commended for their apparent commitment to this school. This commitment is readily evident and shows up in the good rapport between pupils and staff, in the friendly atmosphere that is everywhere apparent, in the lack of vandalism and in the positive support of the school.

2. The efforts of staff and students alike have produced a highly positive humane sort of learning environment in which warm and friendly but forthright interactions take place between teachers and students as a matter of daily routine.

3. The instructional teams have made noteworthy efforts to develop program components and instructional procedures aimed at achieving such desirable objectives as the following:

    a. To meet the needs of individual students
    b. To encourage student involvement in a broad spectrum of learning activities in a multitude of topics and areas
    c. To provide opportunities for students to develop their own individual interests and talents
    d. To structure programs so that all students are required to master a minimum quantity of essential knowledge.

4. Teacher-Advisers have provided leadership in the nine areas of study, and in most cases, together with the para-professional staff, have developed strong instructional teams. The General Aides and Clerical Aides have given support to the total educational structure; and have served, along with the Instructional Assistant, to free professional staff for the more difficult decision-making duties inherent in the teaching-learning process.

5. The staff members are to be commended on the degree of success they have attained in implementing individualized scheduling and pacing. It is recognized that implementation of such approaches requires solutions to a multitude of organizational and technical problems. The staff is working towards this end.

149

Recommendations

1. *Providing individual assistance to students.*

   The procedures used to orient students to the school, to help them choose courses and plan their use of time, and to provide individual assistance to students having difficulty, should be critically analyzed by instructional teams.

   One of the major tenets of the philosophy of this school is that every student must take major responsibility for his (her) own progress (or lack of it). The evaluators found that significant numbers of students had made very little progress toward completing course components in a year of attendance at this school. If the school truly intends to live up to its stated commitment "to provide a program with varied strategies and environments for learning through which all students, regardless of the differences of individual talents and interests may proceed with gains" and if it is to help students learn how to learn, then it must provide students with not only the opportunity, but also the guidance and instruction necessary to employ a wider variety of appropriate learning strategies. Simply offering students choices without giving them training and experience in decision making and planning, so that they can experience wise, effective choices, would seem to be mere window dressing.

   In view of the heavy demands that the counseling role places upon each Teacher-Adviser, it could be beneficial to both students and teachers if alternatives to the individual, teacher-student contact could be found for helping students having difficulties. Additional time for the Teacher-Adviser might be provided by hiring part-time, additional teachers, or by reducing the student-teacher ratio through limiting registrants in the courses. Perhaps utilization of a combination of group and individual procedures, and a variety of activities, resources and learning assignments would open up new possibilities for the development of alternative modes of performing the counseling functions.

2. *Student interaction in small-group sessions.*

   All instructional area teams should try to provide more opportunities for structured, small-group interaction among students

150

for the purpose of using language to gain information, to clarify and revise perceptions and values, and to develop creative and social uses for language.

Small-group seminars should become directly related to the program as found in the unit-paks. Perhaps each unit-pak should contain a few questions which make seminar discussions necessary as part of the credit-gaining process. It may be desirable that the use of unit-paks be an outgrowth of seminars and small-group discussions. They would then become definite research and learning projects rather than information units for credit.

3. *Revision of unit-paks*
   All existing unit-paks should be evaluated thoroughly to determine which one should be discarded, which ones should be revised and to discover components of courses for which entirely new unit-paks must be developed.

   This evaluation of unit-paks should be based upon sets of criteria drawn up by each instructional area team, and should include such general criteria as:

   a. scope and depth necessary to meet adequately the needs of most of the students whether their goals are academic, vocational or personal

   b. emphasis upon the process skills relevant to each of the nine learning areas

   c. an appropriate balance or "mix" of emphases upon the affective and psychomotor domains as well as the cognitive domain

   d. appropriate attention to inquiry and discovery learning approaches as well as to directed acquisition of given knowledge of specifics

   e. structured packages which require students to use a wide variety of learning activities, resources and assignments, compatible with their varying individual needs, interests and capabilities

   f. utilization of diagnostic and evaluating techniques which facilitate individualization of learning and teaching

g. emphasis upon the human interaction components of teaching and learning through provisions of adequate small-group sessions, structured according to the needs of and effective learning styles of different groups of students.

4. *Utilization of resource materials.*

Students should be encouraged to make better use of reference materials and other resources and aides presently in the school.

To this end a central index should be developed of all resources available within the school, and orientation seminars should be given for student use of media. Instructional procedures, including unit-paks, should be designed to encourage greater utilization by students of resource materials on both individual and group basis.

There is a need for more material in terms of texts, film loops, film strips, charts and posters which correlate with the individual instructional unit-paks.

5. *Utilization of human resources in the teaching-learning process.*

The instructional area teams should make a critical analysis of all their present task-experiences with a view to (a) setting up priorities as to which tasks must be completed and which ones could or should be completed, and (b) devising ways and means of utilizing time and resources more effectively to accomplish the high priority tasks.

At present, Teacher-Advisers are unable to do justice to such important tasks as academic counseling of individual students and composing-evaluating-revising courses. There needs to be a greater amount of time spent on curriculum development. The unit-paks are rather incomplete in many instructional areas. A greater emphasis upon cooperative planning among departments might reduce duplication of demand for resources. This recommendation does not preclude the possibility that additional human resources are needed.

6. *Utilization of community resources.*

It is recommended that the coordination of community learning activities be reviewed in terms of:

152

a. What is being done?
b. Who is responsible for it?
c. How is it presently being done?
d. Why is it being done?

The coordination of community-learned activities appears to be a shared function between the Counselors and Teacher-Advisers. Counselors and Teacher-Advisers did not entirely agree as the frequency with which counselors assumed this responsibility. Although community-learned activities is recognized to be an important part of the Model School philosophy, there is an apparent lack of clear understanding as to who has been designed the responsibility for coordinating these activities.

7. *Differentiated staffing.*
The differentiated staffing organization in this school should be continued and further developed.

8. *Communications with public.*
Efforts should be made to improve communications between _____ and its public (Parents, Junior and Senior High Schools, and Universities) with respect to its philosophy, goals, programs, and operation.

9. *Further Study.*
A longitudinal follow-up study should be commenced immediately re the performances of graduates of the _____ _____ in post-secondary institutions. This study should be structured so that it will provide information for use in assessing the quality of the schools' programs.

10. *Finances.*
In order for this school to carry out its operation within the framework of the philosophy of the Model Schools, and in order to achieve its potential, it will be essential that the board provide additional financing.

Within the various reports, there are implications for finances. If these are to be acted on, the above recommendation will have to be considered.

J. CHECKLIST FOR EVALUATING
LEARNING PACKAGES

LP Title and ID No.: _____

Department: _____

Author: _____

Level:
(Circle one)

Basic or
Essential

College Prep or
Pre-Vocational

Enriching or
Advanced

Comments:

The evaluator should check the appropriate box after each *numbered* (required) statement. Even one "unacceptable" check in any required group would render the prescription or package (LP) unacceptable. More than one "needs improvement" check in any required area of the checklist would make the LP questionable.

Unnumbered (supplementary) items are also included in each section, demanding higher than minimal quality (check if present). An LP can be "acceptable" without checking any of these supplementary items. They are listed to provide a basis for greater quality control.

154

A. *Format and Directions*

   1. Title page clearly states the title, identification number (school, department, sequence, etc.) and the level of difficulty (weighting) of the prescription, packet or unit. □ □ □

   2. Title page clearly states the department, subject area and program designation of the unit (Basic, College Prep, etc.) □ □ □

   3. Title page specifies any prerequisities for the unit. □ □ □

   4. Directions and procedures for completing the prescription are clear. □ □ □

   5. Location of special equipment or supplies is clearly detailed or listed on separate information sheet. □ □ □

   6. Learning prescription is neatly typed, gramatically correct, and geared to appropriate reading level. □ □ □

      □ Prescription follows a similar order and sequence to this critique.

      □ Pictures, cartoons, graphs, or colored paper are utilized when appropriate.

      □ Prescription does not exceed 2 or 3 pages.

B. *Concept Focus*

   7. Main idea, skill or attitude is listed in declarative form. □ □ □

   8. Component ideas, skills or attitudes relate logically to the main idea. □ □ □

   9. Component parts are listed in logical sequence. □ □ □

      □ Complex skills are broken down as a series of learning tasks or sub-objectives.

155

C. *Behavioral Objectives*

    10. Objectives specify exactly any conditions required of the student (learning materials, entering behavior, etc.). ☐ ☐ ☐

    11. Objectives specify the learning outcome or behavior, not subject matter, required of the student (verb specifies definite observable behavior). ☐ ☐ ☐

    12. Objectives specify minimum level(s) of student performance. ☐ ☐ ☐

    13. Objectives consistent with the main and component ideas. ☐ ☐ ☐

    14. Objectives reflect the needs and/or interests of the students in relation to the broad school goal. ☐ ☐ ☐

        ☐ Objectives suggest several learning outcomes that reflect the higher levels of taxonomy (analysis, synthesis, evaluation, value systems, etc.).

        ☐ Objectives reflect learning concepts and skills that are applicable to new situations and thinking.

        ☐ Objectives stated precisely so as to be relatively free of overlap.

        ☐ Objectives contain performance criteria from the affective and psychomotor domains (as well as the cognitive).

D. *Multiple Activities, Methodologies and Resources*

    15. Learning activities include a variety of options, materials and media. ☐ ☐ ☐

    16. Required activities are carefully distinguished from the optional. ☐ ☐ ☐

    17. Learning activities are related directly to behavioral objectives and clearly labeled. ☐ ☐ ☐

    18. Some non-print learning activities allow for variations in student learning types (filmstrips, records, tapes, video tapes, charts, etc.). ☐ ☐ ☐

19. Learning activities include a variety of styles and methodologies wherever appropriate (large group, varying small groups, independent study, lab, observation, research, etc.). □ □ □

20. Learning activities achievable within a reasonable period of time (not including remedial work). □ □ □

21. Suggested learning activities include supervised (directed) study for the more dependent learner. □ □ □

22. Content-oriented seminars and discussion groups are required as parts of or following the more significant units (students sign up when prepared). □ □ □

23. Remedial activities are available for students who need additional or alternate work to achieve a given objective. □ □ □

  □ Students instructed to select only those activities they individually need (with teacher advisement).

  □ Performance of any one of several designated activities will lead the student to the specific behavioral objectives.

  □ Learning activities are interesting and enjoyable.

  □ Learning activities permit student-formulated alternatives.

  □ Teacher-prepared materials are available as references or work sheets.

  □ Learning activities are weighted to denote levels of difficulty.

  □ The teacher is listed as a principal resource—at least when an activity requires special materials or guidance.

  □ Suggested learning activities include work experience and/or forms of community service.

157

☐ In at least one activity, the student can verbalize or discuss the components of the unit.

E. *Quest—Suggestions for Breadth and Depth Work*
24. Quest work is listed and is possible at any stage of a unit or following a unit. ☐ ☐ ☐
25. Quest suggestions lead the learner meaningfully beyond the main idea of the unit and are not just busy work.

☐ Quest provides for student formulated alternatives.

☐ Quest work is credited—the academic level and amount is clearly specified.

F. *Evaluation*
26. Pre-test is diagnostic, enabling the teacher to prescribe appropriate activities for the learner. ☐ ☐ ☐
27. Pre-test is an alternate form of the post-test and permits the learner to challenge the unit for credit. (More comprehensive pre-tests are available to permit challenge of a sequence or course). ☐ ☐ ☐
28. Self-test allows the learner to evaluate self-progress and completion of the objectives of the unit. ☐ ☐ ☐
29. Post-test is criterion-referenced, measuring the unit conditions, behavioral objectives and level of performance. ☐ ☐ ☐
30. Alternate forms of evaluation, if required, (oral testing, student self-grading, special projects, etc.) are clearly listed. ☐ ☐ ☐

☐ Self-test is included with the prescription and can be completed and scored by learner without teacher assistance.

☐ An evaluation device is available to permit a student to plot his own progress in the completion of the objectives of the learning prescription.

☐ Post-test includes, whenever appropriate, essay questions in addition to those of the objective-type.

☐ Test items in all forms of summative evaluation frequently reflect the higher levels of the taxonomy.

☐ A critique form is available to permit student evaluation of the effectiveness of a learning prescription or packet.

K. CONTINUOUS PROGRESS MODEL: LANGUAGE ARTS CURRICULUM

Reading	Reading 11 Achievement level: grade 6 and below	Reading 12 Achievement of grade 8 to grade 6	Reading 13 Achievement level of grade 10-8	Reading 14 Advanced Reading Skills Achievement at grade level		
Spelling and Vocabulary	21 Fundamental Spelling and Vocabulary	22 Developmental Spelling and Vocabulary	23 History & Development of the Language			
Oral Communication	Small-group discussion	Oral Composition	Debate			

	41 Practical Composition	42 Theme Development I	43 Theme Development II	44a Expository Writing	44b Expository Writing	45 Advanced Composition	46 Creative Writing
Composition	41 Practical Composition	42 Theme Development I	43 Theme Development II	44a Expository Writing	44b Expository Writing	45 Advanced Composition	46 Creative Writing
Literature	51 Responding to Fiction	52 Responding to Poetry	53 The American in Literature	54 Contemporary Literature	55 Dramatic Literature	56a Literature for College I	56b Literature for College II
Special Courses	61 Survey Mass Media	62 Bible as Literature	63 Mythology	64 Shakespeare	65 Seminar for Advanced Study		

L. PARENT SURVEY

The following data are the result of a year-end survey (1972-73) sent to parents of all students in grades 9-12. 180 questionaires were returned from a possible total of 1150, a 15% return. All figures represent the actual number responding to each item.

1. The Model Schools Project attempts to develop a more self-directed, motivated learner. Do you support this approach to education?

Yes	128
Undecided	33
No	18

2. The *teacher-counselor* helps your student schedule his weekly learning activities, monitors his progress, and confers with parents. Does the *teacher-counselor* plan seem to work for your student?

Yes	114
Undecided	30
No	34

3. The *learning packages* allow your student to work at his own speed. Does this work for your student?

Yes	127
Undecided	23
No	28

4. The learning packages are designed so that your student must master each step of the subject matter before he may advance. Is your student learning the subject matter by using *learning packages?*

Yes	117
Undecided	38
No	22

5. The large-group presentations (LGP) instruct your student and motivate him to work. Is your student motivated by large-group presentations?

Yes	48
Undecided	34

No   96

6. The *small-group discussions* (SGD) allow your student to share his learning experiences with others. Have *small-group discussions* helped your student?
> Yes   77
> Undecided   42
> No   59

7. The goal of the program is to develop your student's ability to *work independently*. Is your student learning to *work independently*?
> Yes   142
> Undecided   19
> No   14

8. Do the materials you receive and teacher-counselor conferences, along with the parent meetings, provide you with the right information about the Model Schools Program?
> Yes   118
> Undecided   21
> No   37

9. Parent conferences provide information on the progress of your student. Were your conferences this year worthwhile?
> Yes   120
> Undecided   22
> No   32

10. How many conferences have you had this school year?
> 0   15
> 1   25
> 2   31
> 3   90
> 4   16
> 5   1

11. Has your student worked in the School of Opportunity *Achievement Center* at any time this year?
> Yes   24
> Undecided   7
> No   142

12. Do you feel that the special programs in the Achievement Center have helped your student become a more self-directed and motivated learner?

    Yes   24
    No Response 156

In which of the following subject areas are you most concerned about your student's progress?

13. Fine Arts (Music, Drama, Art)   19

14. Foreign Culture (Foreign Languages)   44

15. Health, Fitness, Recreation (Phys. Ed.)   10

16. Language Arts (English)   19

17. Mathematics   55

18. Practical Arts (Industrial Arts, Home Ec., Business Ed.)   16

19. Religion   17

20. Science   35

21. Social Science   14

22. Study Skills (Reading)   17

About the Author

When one writes, thinks, or speaks he/she does so from a a position of bias. The objective human is yet to be found. Consequently, the reader of this book should know something about the author, something about the experiences which have made this author what he is and more importantly what he is becoming.

One of these first experiences was my exposure as a graduate student to the Eight Year Study. I read with great interest all the available materials referring to the study and the follow-up evaluative reports. Subsequently, I visited several of the schools which a decade earlier had participated in this exciting project. Disappointment prevailed, for much of the excitement communicated in the literature was not to be found in the schools.

A number of years later I was exposed to several professors in the area of learning theory. Their inputs stimulated further the desire to probe the question, "How do humans learn?" Subsequently, I accepted a part-time appointment with the staff of Daniel Prescott at the University of Maryland in the Institute of Child Study. This exposure both at Maryland and in California gave further insights into the ways persons learn and the importance of providing differing kinds of learning environments.

The gestalt of these experiences caused me to realize the necessity for new approaches to schooling. Without new approaches, schools rarely became humanistic, meaningful environments for learning both affectively and cognitively. Shortly after this gestalt began to form, I had the opportunity of visiting a number of schools which were seeking to implement the concepts developed by J. Lloyd Trump and members of NASSP's committee on staff utilization in secondary education.

Under the leadership of J. Lloyd Trump and at his invitation, I joined the staff of the NASSP-Ford Foundation Internship Project. A combination of Trump's leadership, the inspiration of colleagues such as the late David Beggs from the University of Indiana, my prior exposure to theories of learning and child study—all of these seemed to interrelate and come to fruition through the practical, applied meaningful work of the Model Schools Project.

The author has been a teacher, department head, small school principal, dean of a small liberal arts college, and a university professor. These are merely experiences. Undergirding some 25 years of educational activities has been a a commitment to develop new models for learning. This is an ethical commitment based on my origins in a society whose roots are Hebraic-Christian. The basic tenet of that society is that the individual is essential and critical. The person counts. Systems which treat individuals solely in collective ways are inconsistent with our spiritual and ethical heritage.

This commitment has grown further through my involvement as associate director of the Model Schools Project. Change in schooling is a slow, tedious process. It will demand the total commitment of each and everyone of us. But it will also determine our futures.

William Den Hartog Georgiades

Credits

Many persons and groups contributed to this book.

Earlier reference was made to the essential roles of the National Association of Secondary School Principals' Board of Directors and professional staff members for their suggestions and support.

Also credited earlier were the financial support of the Danforth Foundation and the constructive help of Danforth President Gene Schwilck.

Numerous persons in the Project schools and others who were employed from time to time as professional MSP staff members made suggestions and helped to conduct the studies referred to in this book. Colleagues and graduate students at the University of Southern California also interacted at various times.

Thomas F. Koerner, NASSP Director of Publications and Editorial Services, and Malinda Padgett, Model Schools Project secretary, provided essential help in their respective capacities.

J. Lloyd Trump, MSP Project Director, helped to plan and reacted to the manuscript as it was prepared.